D0849235

BONO

BONO

A Biography

David Kootnikoff

GREENWOOD BIOGRAPHIES

 GREENWOOD

AN IMPRINT OF ABC-CLIO, LLC
Santa Barbara, California • Denver, Colorado • Oxford, England

Library of Congress Cataloging-in-Publication Data

Kootnikoff, David.
    Bono : a biography / David Kootnikoff.
        p. cm. — (Greenwood biographies)
    Includes index.
    ISBN 978-0-313-35509-7 (hardcopy : alk. paper) — ISBN 978-0-313-35510-3
(ebook)   1. Bono, 1960–   2. Rock musicians—Ireland—Biography.
3. U2 (Musical group).   I. Title.
    ML420.B6856K66   2012
    782.42166092—dc23   [B]   2011043805

ISBN: 978-0-313-35509-7
EISBN: 978-0-313-35510-3

16   15   14   13   12   1   2   3   4   5

This book is also available on the World Wide Web as an eBook.
Visit www.abc-clio.com for details.

Greenwood
An Imprint of ABC-CLIO, LLC

ABC-CLIO, LLC
130 Cremona Drive, P.O. Box 1911
Santa Barbara, California 93116-1911

This book is printed on acid-free paper ∞

Manufactured in the United States of America

For Yuko
"The songs are in your eyes"

CONTENTS

SERIES FOREWORD

In response to school and library needs, ABC-CLIO publishes this distinguished series of full-length biographies specifically for student use. Prepared by field experts and professionals, these engaging biographies are tailored for students who need challenging yet accessible biographies. Ideal for school assignments and student research, the length, format, and subject areas are designed to meet educators' requirements and students' interests.

ABC-CLIO offers an extensive selection of biographies spanning all curriculum-related subject areas including social studies, the sciences, literature and the arts, history and politics, and popular culture, covering public figures and famous personalities from all time periods and backgrounds, both historic and contemporary, who have made an impact on American and/or world culture. The subjects of these biographies were chosen based on comprehensive feedback from librarians and educators. Consideration was given to both curriculum relevance and inherent interest. Readers will find a wide array of subject choices from fascinating entertainers like Miley Cyrus and Lady Gaga to inspiring leaders like John F. Kennedy and Nelson Mandela, from the greatest athletes of our time like Michael Jordan and Lance Armstrong to the most amazing success stories of our day like J.K. Rowling and Oprah.

While the emphasis is on fact, not glorification, the books are meant to be fun to read. Each volume provides in-depth information about the subject's life from birth through childhood, the teen years, and adulthood. A thorough account relates family background and education, traces personal and professional influences, and explores struggles, accomplishments, and contributions. A timeline highlights the most significant life events against an historical perspective. Bibliographies supplement the reference value of each volume.

INTRODUCTION

To be one, to be united is a great thing. But to respect the
right to be different is maybe even greater.

Bono

Bono is a reconciler. He was born into conflict, born into a household
where each parent represented a different religious denomination—
Protestant and Catholic. It was during a time and in a place where
such distinctions could make or break an individual. Throughout his
life he's struggled with opposing forces and managed to transcend this
inner conflict to achieve a united vision of purpose. During his early
years, he was determined to be a performer, the lead singer of U2, and
then the band's principle lyricist. In the second half of his life, he has
devoted himself to social issues with the same passion he has for music.

Bono arose from humble beginnings in a middle-class Dublin neighborhood to become the lead singer of one of the most successful rock
bands of modern times. He has also become a passionate antipoverty
advocate, championing various human rights initiatives such as Amnesty International and third world debt relief. He is also a dedicated
son, husband, and father.

Bono's life story is one in which raw spirit overcomes insurmountable odds and is an example for youth from all over the world to gain inspiration from and emulate.

Much of Bono's success is the result of his commitment to changing the world for the better. Bono's optimism has its roots in the Christian faith but it also owes a great debt to the secular salvation offered by rock and roll. Like Bob Dylan or Bruce Springsteen before, Bono's journey to the top has depended on the power of his own convictions as much as on U2's combined talents.

Throughout his career, Bono has expressed the exuberance of youth while facing the challenge of maintaining his integrity during the sometimes murky maturation of becoming an adult. Whether it's the troubles in Northern Ireland, famine in Africa, or AIDS awareness, Bono has helped to illuminate the concerns of his own generation without giving into apathy or cheap cynicism.

TIMELINE: EVENTS IN
THE LIFE OF BONO

May 10, 1960	Paul "Bono" Hewson is born at the Rotunda Hospital in Dublin, Ireland, to Bob and Iris Hewson.
1972	Mount Temple School is established in Dublin and one of its first students is Paul Hewson.
1973	Paul Hewson and Derek "Guggi" Rowen meet Fionan "Gavin Friday" Hanvey.
September 10, 1974	Paul's mother Iris Hewson dies from a brain hemorrhage.
1976	Paul and his friends form Lypton Village. Paul becomes "Bonavox of O'Connell Street" then "Bono Vox" and settles on "Bono."
September 25, 1976	The current members of U2 meet in Larry's kitchen for the first time after responding to a note Larry posted at school about starting a band. They decide to call themselves Feedback.

Autumn/Winter 1976	Feedback plays their first performance in the Mount Temple cafeteria.
April 11, 1977	Feedback plays their first show in front of a paying audience at St. Fintan's School, Dublin. The band decides to change their name to The Hype.
June 1977	The first issue of *Hot Press* music magazine appears.
October 21, 1977	Bono attends the Clash concert at Trinity College in Dublin and is blown away.
February/March 1978	The Hype plays their first RTE broadcast on the program *Our Times*. The band changes their name to U2.
March 18, 1978	U2 wins the St. Patrick's Day contest in Limerick. The prize is 500 pounds and a demo session with CBS Ireland.
March 30	U2 gets their first mention in *Hot Press*.
April	U2 meets *Hot Press* journalist Bill Graham. U2 records their first demo at Keystone Studios.
May 25	U2 meets Paul McGuinness, who soon after becomes their manager.
October	U2 plays the benefit Rock against Sexism at the Magnet Bar in Dublin.
November	Larry's mother is killed in a car accident in Dublin.
April 1979	Bono and Ali travel to London to promote the band.
May	U2 plays the first of six Dandelion Market gigs.
June	U2 signs a contract with CBS Ireland.
September	U2 releases three-song EP *BOY-GIRL*. A thousand copies sell out almost immediately.
October	U2 appears on the cover of *Hot Press* for the first time.
November 10	U2 appears on the cover of *Record Mirror*.

December	U2 embarks on their first tour of England.
January 15, 1980	U2 plays *The Late Show* for the first time.
March 23	U2 signs their first international contract with Island Records.
April 5–6	U2 records "11 O'clock Tick Tock" with Martin Hannett in Dublin's Windmill Lane Studios.
May 23	U2's first international single, "11 O'clock Tick Tock," is released.
July	U2 begins recording their first album, *Boy*, with Steve Lillywhite.
July 27	U2 plays their first open-air concert at Leixlip Castle in front of 15,000.
August	U2 releases their first Steve Lillywhite single, "A Day without Me."
October 20	*Boy* is released and eventually peaks at number 52 on the British charts.
December 3	U2 plays their first show in France at the Baltard Pavilion in Paris.
December 4	U2 flies to the United States.
December 6	U2 plays their first U.S. concert at the Ritz in New York City.
December 9	U2 plays their first show in Canada at the El Mocambo in Toronto.
February 1981	U2 receives first mention in *Rolling Stone* magazine, "Here Come the Next Big Thing" by James Henke.
March 3	*Boy* is released in North America with a new cover and reaches number 94 on the charts.
March 22	Bono leaves his lyric book backstage at a show in Portland.
June 8	U2 plays to 50,000, their largest crowd, at Pinkpop Festival in the Netherlands.
June 9	Bruce Springsteen and Pete Townshend meet U2 backstage at their Hammersmith Palais concert in London.
July	U2 begins recording *October* at Dublin's Windmill Lane Studios with Steve Lillywhite.

July	New single "Fire" is released, peaking at number 35.
August 1	MTV debuts in the United States.
August 20	U2 makes their debut on *Top of the Pops* performing "Fire."
October 5	New single "Gloria" is released, peaking at 55 in the United Kingdom and 81 in the United States.
October 12	New album *October* is released, peaking at 11 in the United Kingdom and 104 in the United States.
November	Edge and Bono quit the band briefly and a crisis of faith occurs. After discussions with Paul, the band reforms with a stronger commitment.
November–December	U.S. tour.
December	U2 records new song "A Celebration" in Dublin.
February 1982	U.S. tour.
February 11	Bono meets photographer Anton Corbijn in New Orleans.
March 4	U2 begins a monthlong stint opening for the J. Geils Band.
March 22	New single "A Celebration/Trash, Trampoline, and the Party Girl" is released.
August 8	U2 begins recording *War* with Steve Lillywhite at Windmill Lane in Dublin.
August 21	Bono marries Alison Stewart at a ceremony in Raheny, Dublin. They honeymoon at Island Record boss Chris Blackwell's property in Jamaica.
December	One-month tour of Europe.
December 15–16	Video shoot for "New Year's Day" in Salen, Sweden.
January 1983	New single "New Year's Day" is released, peaking at number 10 in the United Kingdom.
February 28	*War* is released and reaches number 1 in the United Kingdom and number 12 in the United States.

March	New single "Two Hearts Beat as One" is released.
April 3	U2 records video for "Two Hearts Beat as One" at Sacré Coeur in Paris.
May 21	U2 meets with reps from the Chicago Peace Museum and agrees to contribute materials.
May 30	U2 plays the U.S. Festival.
June 5	U2 plays at Red Rocks Amphitheater near Denver and films it for a future video release.
August	Irish prime minister Garrett Fitzgerald asks Bono to join the Select Government Action Committee on Unemployment.
November 21	*U2 Live—Under a Blood Red Sky* produced by Jimmy Iovine is released, peaking at number 2 in the United Kingdom and number 28 in the United States.
November 22	U2 plays first show in Osaka, Japan.
May	*U2 Live at Red Rocks—Under a Blood Red Sky* video is released.
May 7	U2 begins work on *The Unforgettable Fire* at Slane Castle with Brian Eno and Daniel Lanois.
July 8	Bono interviews Bob Dylan for *Hot Press* and joins him onstage at a Slane Castle concert.
August	U2 films video for "Pride (In The Name Of Love)."
August 1	U2 launches own label, Mother Records.
August 29	U2 plays first show in Christchurch, New Zealand.
September 1	Bono meets Greg Carroll and offers him a job.
September 4	U2 plays first show in Sydney, Australia.
October 1	U2 releases their fourth studio album, *The Unforgettable Fire*, peaking at number 1 in the United Kingdom and number 12 in the United States.
November 25	Bono and Adam participate in the Band Aid recording of the charity single "Do They Know It's Christmas?"
March 14, 1985	*Rolling Stone* puts U2 on its cover with the caption, "Our Choice: Band of the '80s."
May	U2 releases four-track EP *Wide Awake in America*, peaking at number 11 in the United Kingdom and number 37 in the United States.

June 29	U2 plays homecoming show at Croke Park, Dublin, for 57,000 fans.
July 13	U2 plays Live Aid at Wembley Stadium in London for estimated audience of 1.5 billion TV viewers.
September	Bono and Ali fly to Ajibar, Ethiopia, to do relief work.
October	Bono flies to New York to participate in Artists United against Apartheid project Sun City. He meets the Rolling Stones and records "Silver and Gold" with Ron Wood and Keith Richards.
January 1986	U2 begins work on *The Joshua Tree* in Danesmoate House in the south of Dublin with Eno and Lanois.
	Irish band Clannad releases "In a Lifetime" with Bono on vocals.
May 17	U2 headlines Self Aid benefit for the unemployed in Dublin.
June 4	Amnesty International's Conspiracy of Hope tour opens in San Francisco.
July 3	Greg Carroll dies in a motorcycle accident in Dublin.
July 10	Bono, Ali, and Larry attend Greg's funeral in New Zealand.
July	Bono and Ali visit Nicaragua and El Salvador with Central American Mission Partners.
December 14–16	U2 spends three days in the California desert with Anton Corbijn shooting photos for the new album.
March 4, 1987	New single "With or Without You" is released peaking at number 1 in the United States and number 4 in the United Kingdom.
March 9	U2 releases *The Joshua Tree* peaking at number 1 in both the United Kingdom and United States.
March 16	U2 appears on *The Late Show* for a Dubliners' tribute performing "Springhill Mining Disaster."

April 2	*The Joshua Tree* tour opens in Tempe, Arizona.
April 6	Bono meets Frank Sinatra at the Golden Nugget in Las Vegas.
April 27	U2 appears on the cover of *Time* magazine with caption "U2: Rock's Hottest Ticket."
May	New single "I Still Haven't Found What I'm Looking For" is released peaking at number 1 in the United States and number 6 in the United Kingdom.
May 13	*The Joshua Tree* is certified Multi-Platinum by RIAA.
June 2	Bono meets Roy Orbison at Wembley Arena in London.
August	New single "Where the Streets Have No Name" is released peaking at number 4 in the United Kingdom and number 13 in the United States.
September	Director Phil Joanou is confirmed as director of upcoming film, *Rattle and Hum*.
September 26	U2 visits Greater Calvary Baptist Church and meets New Voices of Freedom gospel choir. The event is captured on film by Joanou.
October 12	U2 appears on the Special Olympics charity album *A Very Special Christmas* covering "Christmas (Baby, Please Come Home)."
November 11	U2 plays free outdoor "Save the Yuppies" concert at Herman Plaza in San Francisco.
November 29	U2 records "Angel of Harlem," "When Love Comes to Town," and others at Sun Studios in Memphis.
December 20	*The Joshua Tree* tour wraps up in Tempe, Arizona.
March 2, 1988	*The Joshua Tree* wins two Grammys: Album of the Year and Best Rock Duo or Group with Vocal.
May	Phil Joanou records the band performing "Desire" in Dublin.
June	U2 moves to Los Angeles to finish work on the *Rattle and Hum* soundtrack.
September	U2 appears on the Woody Guthrie/Leadbelly tribute album *Folkways: A Vision Shared* performing "Jesus Christ."

September 19	New single "Desire" is released peaking at number 1 in the United Kingdom and number 3 in the United States.
October 10/11	*Rattle and Hum* album is released peaking at number 1 in the United States, United Kingdom, Australia, and Canada, among other countries.
November 4	*Rattle and Hum* film opens around the world.
December 8	New single "Angel of Harlem" is released peaking at number 9 in the United Kingdom and number 14 in the United States.
January 17, 1989	*Rattle and Hum* is certified Multi-Platinum.
February 1	Roy Orbison's *Mystery Girl* album is released containing Bono and Edge's "She's a Mystery to Me."
April	New single "When Love Comes to Town" is released peaking at number 6 in the United Kingdom and number 68 in the United States.
May 10	First child, daughter Jordan, born.
December 27–30	U2 wraps up the decade with a series of shows at Point Depot in Dublin.
January 17, 1990	Bono inducts the Who into the Rock and Roll Hall of Fame.
February 6	*A Clockwork Orange* debuts in London with music by Bono and Edge.
October	U2 covers Cole Porter's "Night and Day" for the *Red Hot + Blue* compilation.
October 3	U2 travels to Berlin to begin work on *Achtung Baby* with Daniel Lanois.
January 1991	U2 returns to Dublin to finish work on the album.
July 7	Daughter Memphis Eve born.
September	U2 shoots video for "The Fly" in Dublin and London.
September 5	Island Records sues SST Records and Negativland for their single "U2."
October	U2 shoots video for "Mysterious Ways" in Fez, Morocco.

October 21/22	New single "The Fly" is released peaking at number 1 in the United Kingdom and number 61 in the United States.
November 18/19	*Achtung Baby* is released peaking at number 2 in the United Kingdom and number 1 in the United States.
November 24/25	New single "Mysterious Ways" is released peaking at number 9 in the United States and number 13 in the United Kingdom.
February 29, 1992	Zoo TV tour opens in Lakeland, Florida.
March	New single "One" is released peaking at number 7 in the United Kingdom and number 10 in the United States. U2 donates royalties to AIDS research.
June 7/8	New single "Even Better Than the Real Thing" is released peaking at number 12 in the United Kingdom and number 32 in the United States.
June 20	U2 participates in a Greenpeace protest at Sellafield nuclear plant.
September 14	Bono meets presidential candidate Bill Clinton at Chicago's Ritz Carlton Hotel.
December	Bono appears on the cover of *British Vogue* with Christy Turlington.
May 9, 1993	Zooropa tour kicks off in Rotterdam.
June	U2 releases "Numb" as a video single.
June 2	U2 and Island Records announce an extension of the band's current contract, making U2 the highest-paid act in rock history.
July 5/6	U2 releases *Zooropa* peaking at number 1 in the United States and United Kingdom.
July 17	U2 begins including live feed broadcasts from Sarajevo in their shows.
August 11	Salman Rushdie joins Bono onstage at Wembley Stadium in London.
September	New single "Lemon" appears in limited release.
November 5	Bono shoots video of "I've Got You under My Skin" with Frank Sinatra in Palm Springs, California.

November 22/23   New single "Stay (Faraway, So Close)" is released peaking at number 4 in the United Kingdom and United States.

November 26   Adam goes on a drinking binge and misses a concert in Sydney, Australia. Bass technician, Stuart Morgan, fills in.

December 10   U2 plays last show of Zoo TV/Zooropa/Zoomerang tours in Tokyo, Japan.

January 19, 1994   Bono inducts Bob Marley into the Rock and Roll Hall of Fame.

January 25   *In the Name of the Father* soundtrack is released. Bono cowrote the title track and "You Made Me the Thief of Your Heart."

March 1   Bono introduces Frank Sinatra at the Grammys. U2 picks up a Grammy for Best Alternative Album, *Zooropa*.

May 25   U2 earns the Ivor Novello Award for International Achievement.

June 5/6, 1995   New single "Hold Me, Thrill Me, Kiss Me, Kill Me" is released peaking at number 2 in the United Kingdom and number 16 in the United States.

September 12   Bono, Edge, and Brian Eno perform "Miss Sarajevo" and "One" at Luciano Pavarotti's charity concert in Modena, Italy.

September 26   Bono's version of "Hallelujah" appears on *Tower of Song: The Songs of Leonard Cohen*.

November 6/7   *Original Soundtracks 1 by Passengers*, a collaboration between Brian Eno and U2, is released.

December 30   Bono and Ali fly to Sarajevo for the New Year.

May 11, 1996   Bill Graham, the Irish rock journalist and old friend of U2, dies.

February 3/4, 1997   New single "Discotheque" is released peaking at number 1 in the United Kingdom and number 10 in the United States.

March 3/4   *Pop* is released debuting at number 1 in over 30 countries.

April 14/15	New single "Staring at the Sun" is released peaking at number 3 in the United Kingdom and number 26 in the United States.
April 25	U2 opens PopMart tour in Las Vegas.
July 14/15	New single "Last Night on Earth" is released peaking at number 10 in the United Kingdom and number 57 in the United States.
August 12	U2 plays first show in Poland.
September 23	U2 plays historic show in Sarajevo.
September 30	U2 plays first show in Israel.
October 20/21	New single "Please" is released peaking at number 7 in the United Kingdom, but fails to chart in the United States.
December 2	U2's security chief is seriously injured in Mexico City when President Ernesto Zedillo's sons try to get into the concert without an invitation.
December 12	U2 plays last U.S. PopMart show in Seattle.
January 27, 1998	U2 plays Rio de Janeiro, their first South American show.
March 16–21	U2 plays first concerts in South Africa and wraps up 11-month PopMart tour.
May 19	U2 performs in Belfast in support of the Yes campaign for the Irish Peace Agreement.
October 19/20	A new version of "The Sweetest Thing" is released peaking at number 3 in the United Kingdom and number 63 in the United States despite not having a commercial release.
November 2/3	U2 releases first retrospective, *U2: The Best of 1980–1990*, peaking at number 1 in the United Kingdom and number 2 in the United States.
February 16, 1999	Bono helps launch Jubilee 2000 campaign.
March 15	Bono inducts Bruce Springsteen into the Rock and Roll Hall of Fame.
August 18	Son Elijah Bob Patricius Guggi Q born.
September 14	Bono's collaboration with Wyclef Jean, "New Day," is released.

September 23	Bono joins Bob Geldof and other members of Jubilee 2000 to visit Pope John Paul II in the Alban Hills outside Rome.
October 9	Bono helps launch charity concert NetAid at Giants Stadium in New Jersey.
February 9, 2000	Bono attends the premiere in Berlin of his film, *The Million Dollar Hotel*.
March 13/14	*The Million Dollar Hotel* soundtrack is released.
March 18	U2 and Paul McGuinness receive the Freedom of Dublin.
July 18	U2.com opens.
September 7	Bono appears with Nigerian president Olusegun Obasanjo at the UN Millennium Summit to present a petition of more than 21 million signatures calling for debt relief.
October 9/10	U2 releases new single "Beautiful Day" peaking at number 1 in the United Kingdom and number 21 in the United States despite not having a commercial release.
October 30	*All That You Can't Leave Behind* is released debuting at number 1 in 32 countries and number 3 in the United States.
January 29, 2001	New single "Stuck in a Moment You Can't Get Out Of" is released in the United Kingdom peaking at number 2.
February 21	U2 wins three Grammys: Best Rock Group, Song of the Year for "Beautiful Day," and Record of the Year for *All That You Can't Leave Behind*.
March 24	U2 opens Elevation tour in Miami.
May 21	Son John Abraham born.
July 20–21	Bono attends G8 Summit in Genoa, Italy, with Bob Geldof.
August 21	Bono's father, Bob Hewson, dies of cancer.
September 11	Bono is with family in Venice when he watches the twin towers collapse on TV.
October 10	U2 opens third leg of Elevation tour in South Bend, Indiana.

May 16	Bono helps launch DATA's ONE Campaign.
November 22/23	*How to Dismantle an Atomic Bomb* is released, debuting at number 1 in the United Kingdom and United States.
February 13, 2005	U2 wins three Grammys: Best Video, Best Song, and Best Rock Performance for "Vertigo."
February 25	Bono is endorsed by *Los Angeles Times* for World Bank president.
March 14	Bruce Springsteen inducts U2 into the Rock and Roll Hall of Fame.
March 26	Vertigo tour opens in Los Angeles.
July 2	U2 opens Live 8 with Paul McCartney.
December 10	Amnesty International honors U2 with its 2005 Ambassadors of Conscience award.
December 18	*Time* names Bono and Bill and Melinda Gates as their Persons of the Year.
January 25, 2006	Bono attends World Economic Forum in Davos, Switzerland.
February 2, 2006	Bono gives keynote address at National Prayer Breakfast.
February 8	U2 wins five Grammys: Album of the Year, Song of the Year for "Sometimes You Can't Make It On Your Own," Best Rock Song for "City Of Blinding Lights," Best Rock Album, and Best Rock Group.
February 12	U2 opens fourth leg of Vertigo tour in Monterrey, Mexico.
May 16	Bono edits the *Independent* newspaper.
August 29	*Rogue's Gallery* is released with Bono's version of "A Dying Sailor to His Shipmates."
September 22	The book *U2 by U2* is released.
September 25	U2 and Green Day perform a set before a Monday Night Football Game at the Superdome in New Orleans.
November 6	"The Saints Are Coming" is released.
November 7	Vertigo tour kicks off in Brisbane, Australia.
January 1, 2007	"Window in the Skies" is released.

March 1	Bono is honored by the NAACP in Los Angeles.
March 29	Bono receives honorary British Knighthood in Dublin.
May 20	*U2 3D* is screened at Cannes.
September 27	Bono and DATA are honored with Liberty Medal in Philadelphia and he speaks out against torture.
October	Bono appears in film, *Across the Universe*, directed by Julie Taymor.
November	Remastered version of *The Joshua Tree* is released.
June 2008	U2's first three albums—*Boy, October, War*—are rereleased.
January 2009	U2 performs at the We Are One concert held for the inauguration of newly elected president Barack Obama.
January	Bono begins writing column for the *New York Times*.
February 16	New single "Get On Your Boots" is released peaking at number 12 in the United Kingdom and number 40 in the United States.
February 27	U2's 12th studio album, *No Line on the Horizon*, is released peaking at number 1 in the United Kingdom and United States.
March	Paul announces U2 360 stadium tour will begin in the fall of 2009.
October	U2's Rose Bowl concert streamed live on YouTube.
November 26	U2 confirmed headliners at 2010 Glastonbury Festival.
April 2010	*Q Magazine* lists Bono as second-greatest front man of all time.
May	Bono and Bob Geldof edit *Globe and Mail* edition on the future of Africa.
May	Bono injures back in Munich; Glastonbury is canceled and tour is postponed.
August	Bono recovers, tour resumes in Turin, Italy.
November	Broadway Musical, *Spider-Man: Turn Off the Dark*, suffers difficulties and is postponed into the New Year.

Chapter 1

BOYHOOD: ORIGINS AND EARLY DAYS IN DUBLIN

In 1960, the Republic of Ireland was a small nation on the edge of Western Europe without much claim to rock-and-roll fame. Stereotypes of leprechauns and shamrocks overshadowed any true representation of the culture, and it seemed like the last possible location for a burgeoning rock scene. Into this uncertainty was hurled Paul David Hewson, Bono Vox, as he would later be known.

Born in the capital city of Dublin on May 10, 1960, Bono's parents, Iris and Bob, already had one child—seven-year-old Norman. They had been married already for 10 years and had built themselves a modest middle-class life. Bob was a postal worker and Iris took care of the home in a rental house 5 miles outside of Dublin in the suburb of Stillorgan.

Brendan Robert Hewson and Ruth Elizabeth Rankin had lived around the corner from each other before they married in 1950. They were a rare couple for their time. Bob was a Catholic and Iris was a Protestant. Ireland was overwhelmingly Catholic and such interfaith marriages were extremely rare and were discouraged by the Catholic Church. A Catholic who wanted to marry someone from another denomination had to write to the pope for permission. If the marriage was permitted to go ahead, it would take place in a darkened church without flowers or decorations to show the church's disapproval.

Bob seriously considered the prospect, seeking advice from those close to him before deciding on a church ceremony in a Protestant church. Bob and Iris were married on August 19, 1950, and years later a Catholic priest blessed the marriage.[1]

Bob was a huge opera fan and would play such masters as Verdi and Puccini around the house, even singing along in his rich tenor voice. Ruth was an elegant woman, busy in the community and committed to raising her two sons. Norman, the first born, was sent to a Protestant school and attended the same Protestant church with Iris every Sunday, while Bob waited in the car. Norman also took up the guitar and learned to play when Bono was still too young to do so.

When Bono was born it was thought that he would be raised as a Catholic, but when he was old enough he joined Ruth and Norman at the same Protestant church. Religion would always play a central role in Bono's life, and as with everything else, he would seek out his own perspective and interpretation of scripture before committing to any one version. Bob recalled his youngest son's fortuitous fate: "[Iris] went to a fortune-teller and the fortune-teller told my wife that she would have two children and one of them would have the initial P and he would be famous in whatever life he took up."[2]

When Bono was a baby he was loud and demanded attention and he wouldn't stop crying until he received it. It became so bad that Ruth brought him to a doctor to seek a cure but was told there was nothing that could be done. In retrospect, it seemed as though Bono was giving his lungs a workout in preparation for his career as U2's lead singer.

As he grew older, Bono preferred to keep to himself. He would make up characters and pretend to chat with them. When he was in the garden he would pick honeybees off of the flowers and talk with them to make friends. Before intervening, Bob would watch amazed as his youngest son carried on without ever getting stung.

Soon after Bono was born the family moved into the suburb of Ballymun, a mixed neighborhood of working- and middle-class families. For a few years their home was surrounded by fields and trees and Bono and Norman would spend their free time exploring the wilderness right outside their door. This was short lived, however, as the Ballymun towers, the high-rises constructed for lower-middle- and working-class families, went up and changed the neighborhood.

The Hewsons by this time had bought a car and were settling into a comfortable existence, but Bono was uneasy and a bit confused with his own social standing. He couldn't decide if he should identify with the working-class families from the towers or his more comfortable neighbors on Cedarwood Road: "Violence is a thing I remember most from my teenage years and earlier. This was a working-class area that we lived in . . . but you know, the difference between the incomes of people who lived here and who lived there might be very little. It might be, like, a car. My old man had a car, so we were rich. And that was a reason to be tortured."[3]

Bono was enrolled at the Protestant-run Glasnevin National Primary School and became one of the more aggressive boys in his class. On the first day of school when he was only four, he and some other boys were standing outside sharing their dreams for the future. One of Bono's friends said he wanted to be a nuclear scientist and another boy suddenly bit his ear. Bono was furious and grabbed the aggressor's head, slamming it against an iron railing. The crowd dissolved into tears and shouts. It was an early display of Bono's loyalty and his tendency for violence. Despite this incident, Glasnevin also provided him solace and peace: "I used to lie along the banks of the River Tolka, among the flowers—poppies, they were—and just dream. It was a Protestant school. There weren't many protestants in the area, so I had to go out of the area to visit the place. It was a tiny little thing with a tiny little yard. The headmaster was very good to me, to all of us."[4]

After finishing Glasnevin at age 11, Bono switched to St. Patrick's Secondary School for Boys, another Protestant school associated with one of the most prominent cathedrals in Dublin. He had a difficult time adjusting, and his grades fell. Rather than attend the boring lessons he started to skip classes and wander around the center of Dublin. He would walk down Grafton Street and over to St. Stephen's Green, peeking into the pubs and shops along the way. Dublin in the early 1970s could be a rough place, and alcohol, drugs, and crime were always a problem as they are for any major metropolis.

Bono never got into any serious trouble, but he was attracted to the real sights and sounds of the gritty streets, preferring them to the suffocating mediocrity he was enduring at school. Like the artist he would eventually mature into, he knew that the authenticity beyond his schools walls was the stuff of life that provided genuine inspiration.

Bono disliked his school so much that one afternoon at lunch he followed his Spanish teacher, one he particularly disliked, to the park and hid behind a bush as she found a seat. As she began to eat her lunch, Bono picked up some dog excrement and tossed it at her. He was caught, disciplined, and his parents were told of the incident.

Bob and Iris were beginning to be concerned. They saw the changes and were worried Bono could be irreversibly damaging his future. At the same time, he was also making new friends around the neighborhood. Derek Rowan lived nearby and he and Bono had known each other for about four years. As Bono started opening up to the larger world around him, he began to question religion and its place in his own life. Derek and his family were religious, but they weren't Catholic or Protestant. They belonged to a group called the Plymouth Brethren who rejected what they considered the arrogance of religious authorities. The Brethren advocated a direct relationship with God through unmediated understandings of the Bible. Bono was intrigued at first and welcomed the chance to explore an alternative vision of his faith. Soon after, he became a believer.

At home, Bono would try to initiate discussions with his brother Norman and his parents, but they dismissed him saying that 10 years old was too young to understand such issues. This only caused him to go deeper into the Brethren's belief system to gain a fuller understanding for himself. He was uncertain of his family's traditional approach to Christianity and was developing the questioning attitude that would continue throughout his life.

Meanwhile, Bob was realizing that some form of change was necessary for his young son:

Ah, he was exasperating, he really was. But there was nothing bad in him. He was living in his own world and we were sort of superfluous to it. And it still applies today. He was an extraordinary kid. He was very hard to nail down. We couldn't get him to study

when he was in school, just could not get him to study. He'd go off
to study and the next thing you'd hear him strummin' the guitar.[5]

Bob was reading the paper one day when he came across an article
about a new school that had opened called the Mount Temple High
School. It offered a unique approach to education and to Ireland's sec-
tarian conflict. The mission statement of the school announced it was
Dublin's first nondenominational, coeducational secondary school.
Bob thought it would be worth a chance for Bono to turn a new page.

Shortly after, Bono enrolled and he welcomed the school's open-
minded approach and new environment. For the first time in his life
he was together with Catholics and Protestants and was regarded as
an individual first rather than what religion he represented. This was
refreshing for the 12-year-old because he never could decide what religion he truly belonged to—Mount Temple accepted that for once it
was alright to be just a Christian.

Another positive factor was the presence of girls. Bono was at the age
when he was beginning to be interested in girls. Having members of the
opposite sex in his classes helped to balance out his more extreme be-
havioral traits. Another benefit was that Mount Temple didn't require
uniforms and allowed the students to wear whatever clothes they liked.
This appealed to Bono's sense of independence, and he appreciated the
empowerment that came with the responsibility. As a result, he began
to develop his own style and taste. He was confident to be himself,
which led to his increased popularity among his fellow students.

Outside of school, he was also exploring new pursuits, and he became infatuated with chess. He would play with Norman or Bob at
every chance he got and was soon excelling at it. He was so good that
he entered an international competition in Dublin and was the youngest competitor. Although he didn't win the championship, he did
quite well and enjoyed the attention he got for being the youngest.

Chess is a game that requires intense concentration and strategic
planning. A player needs to balance many competing factors at once
while keeping an eye on an opponent's potential moves. It was a challenge that appealed to Bono's intellect and revealed a sophisticated
understanding of strategy from an early age. Later on, Bono drew on

this early training to become a successful communicator and problem solver. He has always been able to quickly grasp the potential of any given situation and appreciate the numerous ways of looking at it.

When music entered Bono's life, chess took a backseat. Music revealed different shades of expression and introduced a more acute awareness of life's dramatic possibilities. It was no wonder that he also took to drama at this time and became known throughout the school as a special character.

Things were going well for Bono and he was well liked by his teachers. He was excelling in history, English, and art and making lots of friends. Around this time he opened up a dance club called The Web in an old schoolhouse on the Mount Temple campus. He gave himself the nickname "Spider" and played both host and DJ. He made a special effort of inviting girls, and the club gave him the opportunity to act out as both a character and a rock performer in front of an audience.

He was a regular watcher of *Top of the Pops* on TV and was dipping into Norman's record collection to listen to the Beatles and Rolling Stones. He was realizing that music had the same power as religion to move people, and he was beginning to understand his own ability to marshal its energy.

At this time he started seeing a girl named Maeve O'Regan and was enjoying his first relationship. At his home Bono's new sense of confidence caused him to assert his identity more forcefully and this generated some problems. He would get into fierce clashes with his father and Norman, and they would sometimes turn violent. His fights with Bob could last for hours. One such incident started after dinner and went on until two in the morning when Bono finally gave in and admitted he was wrong. The next morning, however, he came into the kitchen and announced he had just given up so he could get some sleep. His fights with Norman were physical and sometimes involved bloodshed. He even went so far as to throw a knife at Norman once. Luckily, he missed. Years later he would admit that he "was such a bastard."[6]

In the summer of 1974, Bono's grandparents on Iris's side celebrated their 50th anniversary. It was a big event with members from all sides of the extended family present to share an evening of dinner and dancing. The next day, just as the phone calls and stories were making the rounds, word arrived that Iris's father had suddenly died of a heart attack.

The Hewson household immediately went into mourning and Iris was in a state of shock. How could it happen so unexpectedly? The funeral was set for the beginning of September and once again everyone in the extended family gathered together. Bono had never experienced death before and he too was trying hard to make sense of the incomprehensible. Then at the end of the ceremony Iris collapsed on her way back to the car. At first it was thought she had simply fainted from all the stress and Bob tried hard to revive her, but he was unable to. Iris was rushed to the hospital where she was diagnosed as being in a coma. Bono wasn't sure what that meant or how long she would stay in that condition. The doctors didn't know either, but they informed the family it was just a matter of waiting and seeing.

Four days later on September 10, 1974, Iris was declared dead from a brain hemorrhage. The news sent everyone reeling as they tried to keep from falling apart. Bob struggled to keep the house in order and maintain the routines. Norman was a 21-year-old adult and was more capable of taking care of himself, but Bono at 14 was devastated and it immediately began to affect his emotional life at school. He felt he'd never really gotten to know his mother and was extremely regretful. He also began to resent his home and felt her absence whenever he was there:

> I had a feeling of the house being pulled down on me. My mother died and then there were just three men living on their own in a house. That is all it was then, it ceased being a home. It was just a house with three men killing each other slowly, not knowing what to do with our sense of loss and just taking it out on each other.[7]

He immediately turned to his girlfriend, Maeve, who provided what support she could, and he also reached out to friends at school. He and Derek and an old friend, Reggie Manuel, began to spend more time together away from home. Along with another friend, Fionan Hanvey, they began to hang out during the day at Bono's house when both Norman and Bob were at work. They would listen to music and eat whatever was in the kitchen. When Bob came home after work he would find his home empty but littered with the remnants that Bono's friends had left behind, after failing to clean up after themselves. This went on time and time again and it infuriated Bob.

Bono also had to take on other chores such as the shopping after school, but he would often spend the money Bob had given him on his friends. He also avoided doing the washing as long as he could, sleeping in an unmade bed for weeks before changing the sheets. His confrontations with his father and brother intensified and only drove him further away from the house whenever he got the chance.

The loss of Iris left the household without an organizing force and an emotional center. Bono looked to religion and music to find solace and comfort. At Mount Temple he began to pay more serious attention to his religious teacher, Sophie Shirley. She noticed a change in her student's attitude after his mother passed away. He stopped daydreaming and handing in sloppy work and began to ask questions that revealed some serious forethought. Bono also joined Mount Temple's Christian Union and regularly attended prayer meetings.[8]

Bono was realizing how the Gospels could provide answers and meaning for the questions in his life, emanating from the death of Iris. The appeal of a righteous God who tipped the scales toward justice in the universe was especially comforting and suggested that everything happened for a reason, even the death of a mother. His task was to discover the reason and fulfill his mother's promise.

This trauma in Bono's personal life extended to his girlfriend. After supporting him through the difficult initial phases of his mourning, Maeve decided to put an end to the relationship and began seeing an older boy:

> Maeve O'Regan and I were very close. She too had a boyfriend, a smart lanky long-haired American basketball-playing Neil Young fan who made me feel very inadequate. I felt so square next to my bra-burning brown rice hippie pal. She was ahead of me. Girls of the same age are always much more advanced.[9]

Bono wasn't too hurt by her decision; he was beginning to consider another girl who was a year behind him at Mount Temple. Alison

Stewart had known Bono for a few years already, but she never considered dating him. Ali, as she was known, came from a Protestant family and wanted to become a nurse. She was a beautiful young woman who secretly admired Bono, but she wouldn't allow herself to be charmed too easily or quickly. It would take a few more years before they began a serious relationship.

The music scene in Ireland during the mid-1970s had not achieved much notice from the international press. Bands like Thin Lizzy or musicians like Rory Gallagher were the exceptions. One local group who everyone looked up to was Horslips, Celtic rockers in the mold of prog bands like Jethro Tull who had formed in the early 1970s. They had gained some notoriety in the United Kingdom and Europe, but never in North America.

Bono and his friends were listening to what most Irish youths were into at the time—Peter Frampton, the Eagles, Roxy Music, and lots of David Bowie. Bowie burst on the scene in 1972 with the album *The Rise and Fall of Ziggy Stardust and the Spiders from Mars*, but it was his 1973 album, *Aladdin Sane*, that caught Bono's imagination. The visual imagery was unlike anything around at the time and it spoke directly to his sense of freedom. Bono knew that great artists had to do things differently and knew to shock people from their somnambulistic waltz through life. He had an open mind and was eager to get beyond the top 10 hits or whatever was popular to find something authentically powerful.

The fashion Bono gravitated toward included flared pants or jeans with a sports coat or jean jacket. He wore his hair shoulder length, parted in the middle and feathered on the sides. He would sometimes wear platform shoes with heels. Bono was short and anything that propped him up was a welcome edition.

The conflict in Northern Ireland between Catholics and Protestants known as "the troubles" was in the headlines day after day. It was impossible to escape, even living 105 miles to the south of Belfast, the capital of Northern Ireland. One of the most horrific events known as Bloody Sunday occurred on January 30, 1972, when Bono was still at Glasnevin School. While he was too young to fully understand the causes, it was something he and other children of his generation had to live with and grow accustomed to.

At Mount Temple he realized that religion could be enough to get you killed in the North. Indeed, his parents' mixed marriage probably never could have existed there, nor would he have been able to be as curious or as open minded as he was. He was thankful for the comparative freedom he enjoyed living in the South, but he also was aware that this freedom wasn't absolute. The Catholic Church still exercised much power, and people were constantly being judged based on their religious affiliation.

Bono was also beginning to question why violence was being used by both sides to advance peace. Fighting for peace seemed futile and, indeed, absurd. He began to explore pacifist beliefs and engaged more seriously in political discussions in his history lessons and at home with his brother and father.

Bono had always been a Beatles fan and he loved not only their music but their message of love and their fearless musical explorations on such songs as "Tomorrow Never Knows" and "Strawberry Fields Forever." He was aware that those particular songs were sung by John Lennon, widely regarded as the most politically active and outspoken Beatle. Lennon had also written books, had questioned the relevancy of religion, and had released some powerful songs as a solo performer. Bono wanted to follow his example and make music that did more than sing about romance and love affairs, but also addressed serious issues like politics and religion.

It was around this time that he came across a notice on the bulletin board at Mount Temple asking for anyone interested in forming a band to meet after school at a home in the neighborhood of Artane. On September 25, 1976, Bono joined seven other boys at Larry Mullen Jr.'s home to discuss the possibility of forming a band. He had originally thought he would play guitar. As Larry recalled years later:

> Bono arrived, and he meant to play the guitar, but he couldn't play very well, so he started to sing. He couldn't do that either. But he was such a charismatic character that he was in the band anyway, as soon as he arrived. I was in charge for the first five minutes, but as soon as Bono got there, I was out of a job.[10]

Along with Larry, six students showed up: Adam Clayton, Dave Evans, who would later be known as Edge, his older brother Dick,

Peter Martin, and Ivan McCormick. Adam had the best instrument—he brought along his Ibanez copy of a Gibson EB-3, and Dave and Dick brought along their homemade guitars. Bono tried to pick up one of the guitars, but couldn't pull off anything much more that a few chords that Norman had taught him. He never really had the desire to sit alone in a room and do what it takes to master an instrument. His gift was more to do with interacting socially with others, connecting and transmitting his passions through his voice and gestures. As Larry said, he was always making strong first impressions and he took the band meeting by storm. Bono recalled:

> We were four completely different people, four people going no-where and we decided to go there together. Four rejects, on all different levels, from the system. Four people—four intelligent people—who probably wouldn't be accepted for the ESB or the civil service. The only thing we had in common was the music, but there was, and is, quite an odd unity.[11]

The group hit it off and a consensus emerged about who would form the nucleus of the group. Adam on bass was a natural fit, Dave and Dick had the hardware and the know-how to navigate their way around the guitar, and Bono was as flamboyant and charismatic as any front man could be. Ivan and Peter couldn't play anything so they weren't seriously considered, although they would remain friends and supporters.

Bono immediately stamped his authority on the band and christened them Feedback, because, it was said, that was all they could play. Bono and Adam were in the same grade, a year ahead of Dave and two ahead of Larry. Dick was in his final year at Mount Temple. They began to get to know one another and would meet every week at Larry's place to practice. At first they would knock around popular songs of the day by the Eagles or Rolling Stones until they finally got a chance to perform their first gig at Mount Temple.

At the end of 1976, the school was putting on a talent show and Feedback was slotted to perform two songs, their first-ever public performance. Bono chose one of his favorites, Peter Frampton's "Show Me the Way" and agreed on the Bay City Rollers' "By Bye Baby" for a joke. Bono was always listening to the radio and Frampton's 1976 album was a blockbuster and he was everywhere at the time. Bono honed in on the lyrics, which appealed to his sense of yearning for meaning in a lover or a savior.

On the day of the show they were nervous and worried about whether they could pull it off, if the parts would come together, or if Bono would remember the lyrics. He felt like bouncing off the walls all day and looked wound up as he made his way through the halls to class. They were given the green light to perform outside on a cement platform, sort of like a stage, raised about three feet from the ground. It was a decent outdoor setting for a band. The open sky acted as both a conduit and a release for the combined music and energy of the performers, and Feedback was a hit. Bono fell naturally into his role as a dramatic lead singer raising his arms into the air, moving around the small platform, and fearlessly staring down the crowd. That was one characteristic that always set Bono apart from most other singers—he seemed to be seeking out kindred spirits in the audience, trying to spread the gospel of his music. Adam recalled the event: "It was all over in a flash . . . but in that ten minutes a world opened up of how things could be. At the time I thought a riot had taken place—and maybe it had."[12]

The effect of the concert raised the band's confidence and their status in the school. All five members became instantly popular and were recognized everywhere they went. Bono was already well known and well liked, but his new band gave him something more to invest his time in, something more to believe in. At home, he was studying his favorite lyricists, singing more often with his records, and beginning to write his own lyrics.

Bono was also spending more time with Derek and Reggie. Before Bob or Norm returned home from work, they were still spending time at Bono's playing records and eating food. Sometimes they would skip school and spend the day drifting around the center of Dublin looking for some fun. Eventually, they got tired of looking and decided to make it for themselves.

Bono was searching for new ways to perform. The trio would meet up with Fionan Hanvey and the four of them formed the core of a gang that eventually called themselves Lypton Village. They started doing impromptu performances around the streets of Dublin as a form of performance art:

We invented a Village, which was an alternative community, called Lypton Village, and we used to put on arts installations, when we were sixteen, seventeen, with manic drills and step-ladders. See, the alcohol level in our neighborhood was so high, people going to the pubs a lot, and we were young, arrogant, and probably very annoying kids, but we didn't wanna go that route. The pub looked like a trapdoor to somewhere very predictable, so we wouldn't drink. We used to watch Monty Python. We invented our own language, gave each other names, and we'd dress differently. We would put on these performance-art things, and in the end we formed two bands, the Virgin Prunes and U2.[13]

They began to draw a following and the members adopted nicknames. Hanvey became "Gavin Friday," Derek was tagged "Guggi," and Bono was first dubbed "Steinhegvanhuysen" and then "Bonavox of O'Connell Street" after a hearing-aid shop in Dublin. He didn't take to the name at first and was suspicious about what the Latin referred to. Was it something about high frequencies or deaf mutes? When he learned it meant roughly "good voice," he settled with it as "Bono Vox" and then just "Bono." Dave Evans got the nickname "The Edge" and his brother Dick became "Dik."[14]

Since his mother had passed away three years before, Bono had matured and after some difficult times he had found his calling. He was now a performer, a singer of a five-piece rock band, and was achieving attention and accolades for it. He was also working hard on rehearsals and on preparing for potential gigs. Life had gone from a conflicting conundrum to a much more interesting and engaging endeavor full of passion and challenges.

Another change had been erupting around Mount Temple and Dublin—punk. It had exploded from the Bowery of New York City over the past three years, spread to London's Soho district and, by 1977, had taken the world by storm. Bono had long admired Bowie, one of the forefathers of the punk scene, and he was now hearing the Ramones and the Clash. Like millions of others from his generation, he was being seduced by its raw spirit.

NOTES

1. Martha Trachtenberg, *Bono: Rock Star Activist* (Berkeley Heights: Enslow, 2008), 7.

2. Bill Flanagan, *U2 at the End of the World* (London: Bantam Press, 1995), 525.

3. Michka Assayas, *Bono on Bono* (London: Hodder & Stoughton, 2005), 112.

4. Ibid., 111.

5. Tony Clayton-Lea, *U2 Popaganda: Essential U2 Quotations* (Dublin: Hodder Headline Ireland, 2007), 227–228.

6. David Schaffer, *Bono* (New York: Lucent Books, 2004), 19.

7. Clayton-Lea, *U2 Popaganda*, 237.

8. Schaffer, *Bono*, 20.

9. Assayas, *Bono on Bono*, 115.

10. Schaffer, *Bono*, 23.

11. Clayton-Lea, *U2 Popaganda*, 229.

12. *U2 by U2* (New York: HarperCollins, 2006), 32.

13. Assayas, *Bono on Bono*, 114.

14. *U2 by U2*, 39.

Chapter 2

TWILIGHT: WIDE AWAKE

All the new attention the band was getting motivated the boys to seek out more gigs. Throughout January and February 1977 they began rehearsing more at Adam's place in Malahide, trying to build their repertoire with more songs by the Eagles, Chuck Berry, and the Rolling Stones. Bono was gaining in confidence at the mic and the rest of the band was beginning to understand each other's styles. Adam knew he would need to work with Larry to become a single-rhythm section while Edge was making more stabs at lead licks, and Dik played rhythm. Bono would sometimes pick up the guitar as a prop and strum along while singing, but it was a distraction and acted as an obstacle between his vocals and the emotional core of the song. He didn't realize it at the time but a lead singer needs to know he can rely on his band to hold things in place while he prepares to take off and return for a landing. All these dynamics were being worked out in these early months, whether or not the band was conscious of them.

During Easter 1977 they got another chance to play live, their second-ever gig, at St. Fintan's, a high school in North Dublin. It was to be their first paying gig and the band was excited. They sat down and worked out a solid set list they thought drew on a wide array of

influences to showcase their versatility. Bono was eager for more experience and was hungering to play live. Feedback was a last-minute ad-
dition to the bill after another band failed to come through. The boys
were given the opening slot, usually reserved for the youngest or least
well-known group, but they didn't care—at least it paid.

The night of the concert rolled around, and the band arrived at the
venue in plenty of time. They were to play along with two other local
groups, Rat Salad and the Arthur Phybbes Band. They took the stage
in the small, dimly lit auditorium and played a set that stretched for
40 minutes and included two female singers, friends from Mount Temple, as backup singers and another on flute. Their set included Chuck
Berry's "Johnny B. Goode," the Eagles' "Peaceful Easy Feeling," Frampton's "Show Me the Way," and the Moody Blues' "Nights in White
Satin." Unfortunately, their ambitions couldn't keep pace with their
talents. Bono had been singing through a guitar amp and his voice
was louder than the music. The changes were sloppy and the tempo
throughout was unsteady. Some members in the audience were laugh-
ing, while others lost interest quickly and gave up trying to listen with
any interest. Nevertheless, the gig didn't dampen their enthusiasm or
resolve, and it actually solidified more fans who admired the band's
determination and conviction.

Bono, however, was shaken by the poor reception. He was prone
to high emotional states that could also plummet under poor circumstances. He had had very high hopes for the gig and had worked hard,
preparing by first carefully choosing the set list with the rest of the band
and then making sure he had all the lyrics memorized. But as soon as
the band made it through the first few bars of their set, he sensed something wasn't right. He couldn't hear much of the bass or guitars, and
he didn't feel as in control of his vocals as he did in rehearsals. By the
second song, he could see the audience losing interest and not respond-
ing to his dynamics. Instead of smiles or applause, he was getting scoffs
and silent stares.

They packed up their gear, collected their pay, and went home.
Within a few days, Bono had turned his attitude around and was
ready to play again. He and the band had learned a valuable lesson about the difference between playing live in front of a group of
strangers and rehearsing alone in a room. Live performances are very

unpredictable and volatile affairs. Sometimes no matter what you do, nothing seems to go right. At other times, you know things will go well the moment you step on the stage. Of course, the more experience you have, the better you can prepare and exert a bit of control, but even the most seasoned pros have off nights. This was an important lesson to learn.

Another lesson he was learning was something more basic about the transformation that occurs when a performer steps in front of people. Amateurs make the mistake of believing they don't need to be fully prepared before going live, that the feeling they had in a room by themselves or in front of their bandmates will be replicated when they step onto the stage. This rarely ever happens. Something changes the moment the element of an audience, a group of strangers, is introduced. The singer will suddenly feel a sense of self-consciousness he never felt before, confidence will slide, and memory will fade. Bono was learning the truth behind the old cliché, "practice makes perfect." A performer needs to be so prepared that everything is memorized not only at a conscious level but also on the unconscious level so that the performer can access the zone, that state of being where everything is in sync and naturally flows without the performer, or sometimes the athlete, thinking about doing it. The band doubled down and worked harder than ever before after the St. Fintan's setback.

The Lypton Village remained a potent force in Bono's life, and he was also attending regular prayer meetings. He was aware of the debauchery that many other rockers celebrated and glorified, and the prayer meetings confirmed his resolve to act differently. He was also writing songs more frequently and trying to address issues that were going on around him and inside his head. He brought "What's Going On?" to the band and they rehearsed it, oblivious to who Marvin Gaye was or that the title of one of Gaye's biggest hits shared the same name. Bono was asking questions about what was bothering him—the politics of violence, apathy, sex, religion.

All through the spring and summer, the band rehearsed at Adam's place and threw new songs into the mix. The band decided they needed a new name and settled on The Hype. Bono was seeing Ali now, after she finally relented and felt she could trust him. They spent a lot of time together at school, and as spring blossomed all around Dublin, the couple was a regular fixture in the coffee shops and around the downtown area.

A few of the songs the band was learning were the Eagles' "Hotel California" and the Rolling Stones' "Jumpin' Jack Flash." They were rock standards that most bands tackled and audiences instantly recognized them as worthy classics. Bono's influences were mainstream at this point, and the band wasn't agile enough to take any chances or branch out into unknown territory. They were still amateurs but with a bucketful of enthusiasm.

Bono was still performing with Lypton Village around Dublin's streets and also attending meetings held by the Plymouth Brethren. The group traced its origins to the 1820s in Dublin before it spread wider to Britain and the rest of Europe. It lacks a central hierarchy and refers to the Bible as its sole guide in matters of faith. As a result, it has no clergy and no doctrine apart from the Bible, although it does accept baptism and communion as its only two ordinances. Bono looked forward to the Brethren's weekly meetings where he could engage with other believers directly without feeling he might be transgressing the laws of a church or unknowingly offending the tenets of the faith. He read his Bible and was prepared and eager to discuss incongruities or ambiguities as he saw them so he could determine a way to reconcile his faith with it and not through some intermediary. The process was fulfilling and it set the stage for the evolution of his spiritual beliefs for the rest of his life.

In June, Bono wrote his exams and finished his five years at Mount Temple. He was leaving Larry, Edge, and Ali behind, but Adam had recently been kicked out after getting caught running through the halls stark naked. Nevertheless, he was granted his graduation papers because he was so close to the end of the final year, but the incident remained a source of embarrassment. Bono had applied and was accepted at University College Dublin in September. Bob was a bit skeptical that his son was really serious about a university education, but he thought it only fair to let him try. He agreed to pay all his expenses for the first year, and if Bono remained committed he would continue to support him. If not, he would have to get a job. Bono agreed.

Throughout the summer, the band continued rehearsing, and although they were working on classic rock songs, the new sounds of punk were swirling all around throughout Dublin in the summer of 1977. Around this time, Adam traveled to London to work for a few weeks, and when he returned to Dublin he had stories, new fashions, and records to share. He had picked up records by the New York City punk pioneers Richard Hell and Patti Smith, and the rest of the band soaked up the new sounds like sponges. Larry was the only one who wasn't impressed. The street ethic and what he thought was the emphasis on raw violence turned him off. He couldn't understand why the musicianship was so basic and simple. He was still listening to the Eagles and Bruce Springsteen and would need more convincing before his tastes would change. The punk sounds from London had already made their way across the sea, and the band was familiar with such bands as the Sex Pistols, the Damned, and the Clash. The band resisted emulating it, however, thinking that punk was a fad that was contrived to sell records.

At the end of the summer, it was time for everyone to get busy with school, or work in the case of Adam. Bono began college, but after a few weeks he was informed that there had been a mistake with his application. For some reason the college had overlooked the fact that he had failed Irish at Mount Temple, and as a result he would have to withdraw immediately. He had no choice, and within a few days he made the decision to return to Mount Temple to work on his Irish. He was actually very relieved to postpone any college for a while, and the setback turned into a perfect opportunity to pursue music and be with Ali.

That October the band secured another gig at the Marine Hotel and then unveiled their new set list with a brand new batch of covers. It was a strange venue, small and cramped, and the crowd seemed to be uninterested in hearing any live music. Nevertheless, their hard work paid off, and they played better than their previous spot at St. Fintan's. Still, Bono knew something wasn't quite right. This time it wasn't his lack of preparation or any sloppy changes or wrong notes. The level of passion and intensity he could feel for the music wasn't as real or as authentic as he knew it should be. When he raised the issue with the rest of the band, they couldn't understand at first. Despite the crowd, they were feeling pretty good about their performance and didn't share Bono's views. What if the music was original, Bono suggested, what if the songs came from within each member, then they would all have a personal stake, one much more intense than covering other people's songs:

> When we started off as a group, the last thing we wanted was to sound like anyone else. In fact, we rejected rock and roll in the old sense. . . . We really rejected it because so many bands back there on Baggot Street in the strip in Dublin were playing this music into the ground. With U2 we wanted to develop an original sound and bring a new point of view to rock and roll, and I think we've done that.[1]

Once again, Bono proved to be right. The rest of the band couldn't deny his main point. Yes, they had sounded better, yes, they were improving, but imagine how much better they could be if the songs were their own! Bono was developing a deeper understanding of his art and what it took to make a band great. Dublin was overflowing with cover bands—every pub had a group that tried to play the Stones, Slade, or Eagles. It made no sense to try and follow them if they were serious about being the real thing—an original rock band.

In the fall of 1977, the Clash's "Get Out of Control" tour came to Trinity College in Dublin. Bono made sure to check it out. He was blown away and later said it turned his world upside down:[2]

> It wasn't so much a musical event. It was more like the Red Army had arrived, on a cold October night, to force feed a new cultural revolution, punk rock. Marching boots and the smell of sulphur. Not weed or speed but fear, fear of the future, no future. And the delight, so much delight. All kinds of symbols pinned on jackets, some ridiculous swastikas, Red Brigade t-shirts, hand made knock-offs of extremely expensive Seditionaries threads from London. But as there was a war going on 100 miles from here, in a strange way, the Clash made more sense in Dublin than anywhere.
>
> As I sat in the box room and stared out the window the next day, it was very clear. The world is more malleable than you think; reality is what you can get away with.[3]

The Clash's expression of punk was more appealing to Bono than the Sex Pistols. It seemed less contrived and more sincere than the Pistols, and the Clash's message was ultimately more hopeful. They too wanted to challenge the status quo and trash hypocrisy, but they also espoused putting power into the hands of people to bring about real change. Bono thought the Pistols' message was too nihilistic, violence for the sake of violence that didn't amount to anything but destruction. The truth was the Pistols were more thorough in their contempt for hypocrisy and targeted religion just as fiercely as they targeted the Queen of England. Bono not only found the imagery of the anti-Christ gratuitous but felt that it was a step too far. The message of Christ was too close to his heart to mock.

That night at Trinity confirmed what Bono had thought about performing original material. The Clash delivered their set with the conviction of revolutionaries storming the Bastille, and all their material was original. Bono saw how the effect on the crowd was undeniable. The assault was total and complete—nothing fancy was needed, no big arrangements or long-winded solos; as Joe Strummer had put it, instinct over intellect. The execution was simple and immediate, but the purpose was as intellectual as German philosophy. Bono knew his band could do the same if they wrote their own material and addressed the same social issues the Clash did that night.

After the gig, Bono began to experiment more with his style and he looked to Iggy Pop's recent release for inspiration. *The Idiot* was regarded as Iggy's comeback album and an attempt to address the punk scene. He was older than those in the scene but he, along with Lou Reed and David Bowie, was revered as one of the godfathers of punk. He had already been playing raw rock and roll since his debut with his first band, the Stooges, in 1969. Bono liked the idea of wearing a suit in the context of punk. It added an element of sophistication to the yobo leanings of the scene. Bono even went so far as to try wearing a safety pin in his cheek. When he showed up at Mount Temple, Ali was shocked and threatened to break up with him. Bono laughed and took it off—it hadn't been real.

At home, Bob was as concerned as ever that Bono was frittering his time away and not taking anything seriously. Bono was supposed to be considering a career or a profession and yet he was still at high school for only one course and staying out at all hours in the evenings. Bob watched in horror while his son started going by a different name and changing his style of clothes and hair to look like a freak. Bob was not only a traditional Irishman—he was also a man's man and he viewed rock stars as effeminate slackers who contributed little to society. He was horrified that his own son not only admired them but seemed intent on following their depraved example.

Bono wasn't oblivious to this tension and tried to avoid conflict as best as he could by timing his comings and goings at his home around Bob's schedule. Norm and Bono clashed periodically and sometimes it rose to levels of fisticuffs. For the most part, however, both brothers respected their differences and kept out of each other's faces. Norm had his own life and job and was trying to work toward moving out of the family home and build himself an independent future.

In rehearsals, Bono was playing little guitar and leaving it to the Evans brothers to flesh things out. He was doing some writing on his guitar at home, and he would share the chord changes and lyrics with the band to develop the melody and song. They finally emerged with two serious attempts called "The Fool" and "Street Missions." Musically, both took early Bowie as their template and fused it with the languorous stadium rock of local heroes Horslips. "The Fool" was loosely based on the concept of the mask Bono was familiar with from his drama lessons. He adopted a naive persona to write the lyrics, and when he sang it he became that character.

Part of his inclusion in Lypton Village involved agreeing to certain tenets. One of these was the idea that members revel in their innocence and wonder and approach the world as though they were still children. The world as it was discouraged innocence, and the way to rectify it was to go out in the streets and act out moments of wonder, be courageous enough to be the fool.

"Street Missions" confronted the idea espoused by the Brethren that churches and gospels could originate from the streets among the downtrodden and still be celebrated as God's word. Bono was applying all the lessons he had learned from his favorite sources and putting them into his art. As a result, he was inspiring the others in the band. That they were growing in confidence and working on their own songs proved to be a true motivator for overcoming the boring routines Bono had been reacting against.

In the winter of 1978, The Hype made their first-ever appearance on the RTE TV program *Our Times*, performing "The Fool." It was a huge boost to their prestige, and other local bands began to take notice. Steve Averill was an ex-member of the Dublin band the Radiators, and he suggested the name U2 to Adam. When the rest of the group heard it, they weren't immediately convinced they needed to replace The Hype. Adam wanted the new name, and Bono started to come around. Both were fans of the British new-wave band XTC, and U2 was easy to remember. It also implied a collective effort as in "you, too," which Bono liked. After a few weeks of pondering, it was decided— they would from then on be known as U2.

The TV performance opened up new opportunities, and in March, on St. Patrick's Day, the band drove to Limerick to participate in a Harp Lager competition. They had to leave Dik behind, but the rest of the band wasn't too worried, and Bono felt some relief. He'd been thinking for some time that Dik wasn't fitting into the band and was out of place. Dik was also missing rehearsals and didn't appear to be as serious as his younger brother. Edge knew it was just a matter of time before Dik quit or was kicked out, but he wasn't so sure that his own skills would be enough to make up his older brother's absence.

In Limerick, he was proved wrong. U2 advanced to the final round and the band had to spend the night in Limerick. They hadn't expected to win, and Mr. Evans, who had driven the van for the band, found a hotel and they tucked in for the night. The band was dumbstruck. They never believed they would advance this far and didn't bother making plans to stay the night. Bono phoned Bob and Ali, elated and excited about the band's performance.

The next day U2 was still walking on air and felt they had already won by getting into the finals. They then performed and won, earning a trophy and a recording session with CBS Ireland. It was a definitive moment and convinced the band that with hard work they could achieve anything it took to succeed. The new Irish music magazine, *Hot Press*, even had a write-up about the win: "Newly-formed Dublin New Wave band U-2 scored a blow for rock 'n' roll when they won the top prize of £500 in a group contest co-sponsored by the *Evening*

Press and Harp Lager held recently during the Civic Week in Limerick. That's what you call getting the breaks."[4]

Jack Hayden was the CBS representative and he arranged to go to Dublin's Keystone Studios with the band a few weeks later. It was an unbelievable opportunity, and Bono felt as though his dreams were being vindicated. When they entered the studio, the band was overwhelmed with the technology and all the potential it suggested. Hayden tried to make them feel at ease, but they were all neophytes and couldn't settle down or relax. The results were less than stellar. They weren't sure enough of themselves to take control of the sessions and being only 17 and 18 they couldn't really be expected to.

Afterward, Bono recognized the band's limitations when it came to recording, and he tried to encourage the others to take an interest in technological matters. Edge had always been interested in audio sonics, and had built his own guitar with Dik when he was younger. He had a natural predilection for creating novel sounds and took a serious interest in it.

Shortly after their victory in Limerick, they bumped into the RTE producer of the TV program called *Youngline* at Mount Temple. He was there to invite the school choir to perform on the show. Bono introduced himself and began raving about U2's prodigious skills. The producer agreed to let them audition; the band played a few Ramones' covers and was booked. On the show they played "Street Missions" and an original Edge had written called "Life on a Distant Planet." They pulled it off without any glitches, although Bono did appear to be a bit overly dramatic in his presentation. The band's visual appearance looked anything but punk, despite their recent forays and interest in bands such as the Ramones and the Clash. Bono was wearing flared white pants and had feathered his hair in the style of teen heartthrob David Cassidy.

Bono has always marched to the beat of a different drummer and been an iconoclast at heart. Even though he was a fan of punk, and even sang cover versions, he didn't feel that he had to dress the part or follow any orders to conform. The same has always been true of U2, and it explains their long-term appeal among their fans. No band sounds like U2, and apart from a few riffs on their first couple of albums, their sound is unique. Their musical precedents weren't really punk but post-punk bands such as PiL and the Gang of Four. Still, U2's DIY ethos shared the same spirit as punk.

While U2 was winning competitions and recording, members of Lypton Village, friends like Guggi and Gavin, had formed a gothic-rock band called the Virgin Prunes with Edge's brother, Dik. They had stopped doing as many street performances as everyone seemed to be seriously at work on their own projects. The Village still got together and shared their own coded language and would soon begin playing together at gigs around Dublin.

Adam had much free time on his hands and he put it to good use. He called up local legend Phil Lynott from Thin Lizzy and asked him for advice about how to make it in the business and secure gigs around Dublin. One thing U2 needed above all was a manager who would work exclusively on these tasks and leave the band free to write and perform. They were also making contacts in the press, specifically journalist Bill Graham, who was writing for *Hot Press*.

In May, U2 was booked to play Dublin's Project Arts Center and Graham invited a friend, Paul McGuinness, along. McGuinness was 10 years older than Bono, was English, and had some prior experience in managing a band. He was looking for a new project and U2 fit into his plans. He was impressed and noticed that Bono's stage presence was particularly electrifying in the way he was reaching out to the crowd with his eyes and gestures. Bono clearly had something to share and something he wanted to say. Paul and the band hit it off and they agreed to work together:

> I wanted to manage them because I thought they could be a very big group. There are bands who legitimately wish to do nothing more than play a weekends, and there are other bands who implicitly want to do what great bands have done, and I suppose U2 were always in that category. They always wanted to be a great band, and it was clear from the beginning that anything short of that was going to be a disappointment. We were sanguine enough I suppose in the beginning to know that the odds against that were very high but we were all nonetheless prepared to try.[5]

Shortly after, Larry, Edge, and Bono graduated from Mount Temple and decisions had to be made about what they were to do in their futures. Bob could see that his son's band was getting somewhere and agreed to give him one year to secure a record deal or he would have to move out. Larry had to get a job and found one with an oil company, but soon he was missing rehearsals. Bono and the rest of the band were getting concerned and had discussions about replacing him, but when they confronted Larry with the problem he agreed not to miss any more rehearsals.

Bono had always been looking for ways to engage with social and political issues, and U2 got their first opportunity to play a benefit concert in support of the Contraception Action Campaign's attempt to allow for the free availability of condoms in Ireland. Bill Graham reviewed the band that August: "U-2 owe no obvious debts to earlier styles. Their songs are uniquely their own, vibrant celebrations that are both direct in impact yet not so simple in style."[6]

More original songs were added to their set list such as "Out of Control" and "Shadows and Tall Trees" that would eventually be included on their debut album. In September, U2 got their biggest break playing to a crowd of 2,500 in Dun Laoghaire's Top Hat Ballroom, backing veteran punkers the Stranglers. There was some confusion and anxiety when U2 wasn't able to secure a sound check or a dressing room. Paul wasn't able to make the gig, and the band felt they were not being given a fair shake or professional treatment.

Bono tried to connect with the Stranglers and sought out the individual members during the evening to speak with them. They weren't interested and snubbed the younger performer, much to his chagrin. He persisted and got into a furious argument with bassist Jean-Jacques Burnel after accusing the older band of an elitist attitude that had nothing to do with punk. He then finally broke into their dressing room and stole a bottle of wine.

As the gigs became more frequent, Bono invited the Virgin Prunes to open for them. By this time the Prunes had developed a confrontational show that involved performing simulations of sex onstage, which they referred to as "Art-F***." Paul was worried that the two bands were becoming incompatible, drawing on different crowds, and suggested they go their separate ways. Bono resisted at first, not want-ing his best friends to be barred from opening up for U2.

Paul was asserting more control and providing U2 with much-needed direction. He arranged for Horslips' lead singer and bassist, Barry Dev-lin, to produce another demo at Keystone Studios. It included "Street Missions," "The Fool," and "Shadow and Tall Trees." Paul sent it to record labels in London, but nothing came of it. Just as the band was waiting for a response, tragedy struck Larry when his mother was killed in a car accident. Bono knew what Larry must have been going through and immediately reached out to offer his support and advice. He knew that it was a traumatic time and although Larry was at a different stage in his life than Bono was when his mother had died, there were simi-larities. He invited Larry to prayer meetings with Edge, and they at-tended other gatherings organized by a Christian group similar to the Brethren called Shalom.

The demo didn't succeed in generating the response U2 desired, but still the gigs kept coming and they continued to generate a buzz around Dublin. In December, they backed up another gang of punks, the Greedy Bastards, consisting of former Sex Pistols Steve Jones and Paul Cook and Thin Lizzy's bandleader, Phil Lynott. U2 was beginning to realize that they shared little with punk as it looked in December 1978. The scene had moved past its heyday and was now degenerating into an excess of drugs and alcohol, basically self-destructing. The Bas-tards' show wasn't impressive and Bono was turned off by their sloppy approach. Steve Jones even forgot his guitar and had to borrow Edge's precious Explorer.

Bono was listening to the other Sex Pistol—Johnny Rotten—now going by his real name, John Lydon. After the Pistols broke up, Lydon went on to form a new band, Public Image Ltd., with guitarist Keith Levene. They had developed a new sound referred to as post-punk, which was heavily influenced by Krautrock bands Neu! and Can and American bands such as Captain Beefheart's Magic Band and Pere Ubu. PiL had just released their first single in October, "Public Image," and it was generating a huge buzz. Bono liked what he heard. He dis-cussed it with Edge and they zeroed in on Levene's unique guitar sound. Bono encouraged Edge to continue to develop his own signature style that he had been exploring. Bono suggested Edge buy a Memory Man delay unit emphasizing that he wanted to keep things spontaneous and open to different shifts in tempo or mood. Punk was too blunt and restrictive; post-punk offered the promise of developing new approaches without any limitations. When Edge plugged into the delay unit he knew he had something special. Soon he was developing his own style such as using two notes rather than three to form open chords.

As 1979 approached, U2 was getting increasingly frustrated about not getting a break from a record label. Bono was feeling the pressure with the passage of time because he knew his father was ready to kick him out of the house if his prospects didn't improve. If that happened, he would have to get a full-time job to survive, and his dreams of leading a band would be finished. He eventually decided to take matters into his own hands and arranged a trip to London to try and stir up some attention for the band. In April, he and Ali spent a week going around to magazines such as *Sounds, New Musical Express,* and *Record Mirror,* dropping off their demo and trying to generate some interest. It was the first time Bono and Ali had spent a week alone without the interference of family and friends and they hit it off. They were serious about each other and had spoken about marriage but first needed to achieve careers or at least get on a path that would lead to something they could be satisfied with.

After they returned to Dublin, they confessed that nothing substantial had occurred—no major breakthrough or feature stories. London was still regarded as the center of the universe and a young band from Dublin without major label interest wasn't taken very seriously. Moreover, if the lead singer had to do the publicity, then they obviously still had a ways to go. Nevertheless, Bono made a lot of contacts which made it easier in the future when things would hopefully look better for U2.

In May, U2 finally got a coveted regular gig every Saturday at Dublin's Dandelion Market. It was another high-profile spot that helped further solidify their reputation in the city. Bono had recently met a local celebrity, Mannix Flynn, who was well known in theatrical circles, and he agreed to help teach the young singer some tricks of the trade to use onstage. He pointed out the importance of grand gestures, of overexaggerating certain moves so those at the back of the crowd could see what was going on. Bono also learned the importance of voice projection and eye contact. Mannix pointed out that the connection with the audience was essential, more so for a band performance than a drama, and he coached Bono to pick out certain people in the audience who looked engaged and play to them.

In June, Paul's hard work paid off and two CBS representatives from London agreed to come to Dublin to hear U2 perform at McGonagle's pub. The representatives liked what they heard and agreed to finance a three-song demo at Keystone Studios with Chas de Whalley and a mixing at Windmill Lane Studios. Once again the band wasn't happy with the results, and de Whalley suggested Larry was the problem. He went so far as to suggest that the band drop him. They refused and took the demo to Dave Fanning, a local DJ with a popular radio show:

> 1978 was the first I'd probably heard of U2 and I got involved because I played their demo tapes, and they were one of those bands that I was trying to help along. . . . Looking back it's very easy to say, "Oh, we all knew Bono had it." No, we didn't. But we certainly knew he was a bit more of a chancer, which is what was needed.[7]

Fanning interviewed Bono who was intent on setting U2 apart from other Irish bands such as the Undertones, and he refused to let U2 be categorized as a punk or new-wave band. Fanning did the band a huge favor when he asked his listeners to get involved and choose what song from the three demos should be the A-side for an upcoming release. The choice was "Out of Control" and the U23 EP came out in September with "Stories for Boys" and "Boy/Girl" on the B-side. Only 1,000 copies were pressed and they sold out within days.

Following this success, *Sounds* magazine did a feature on U2 and *Hot Press* featured U2 in their October cover story titled "Boys In Control." The next month *Record Mirror* followed. Bono began nagging the rest of the band to consider a tour, but Edge had recently enrolled in a technical college to appease his parents and wasn't able to take any time off until his break in December. Paul went ahead and booked a two-week December tour of England, but at the last minute the financing fell through and their parents had to donate some money to make it a reality.

When they arrived in London, they were excited but also daunted by the huge task awaiting them. U2 was booked into Dingwalls and the Moonlight Club and backed up synth-pop band Orchestral Manoeuvres in the Dark and the Talking Heads. The weather was dreary and cold and the living conditions were cramped, but it was only a week. The tour had succeeded in helping the band make connections and exposing them to a higher level of professionalism, but they were still without a record deal.

On their return to Dublin, Bono suggested a homecoming concert, and Paul booked the National Stadium, with a capacity of 2,500, for February 26. Only about 1,000 tickets sold, but it fostered the impression that the band had grown since returning from London. They also arranged for Island Record's Nick Stewart to attend, and after the gig he finally offered them a deal. When Bono told his father, he was surprised and cautious. He knew the deal could collapse or lead to nowhere. The next month the band was invited to London and on March 23, 1980, they signed their first-ever contract. It was for four albums in five years and included 100,000 pounds and 50,000 pounds for both recording and touring expenses.

Bono was elated. All their hard work and sacrifice had been worthwhile. The band would soon be releasing their debut album with support from a label that had a reputation for quality. Originally started by Chris Blackwell, Island had been known to take chances that paid off, specifically on Bob Marley. Bono couldn't have been happier.

NOTES

1. Tony Clayton-Lea, *U2 Popaganda: Essential U2 Quotations* (Dublin: Hodder Headline Ireland, 2007), 232–33.

2. Matt McGee, *U2: A Diary* (London: Omnibus Press, 2008), 12.

3. "25 of the Greatest Gigs Ever," *Guardian*, January 21, 2007, http://www.guardian.co.uk/music/2007/jan/21/popandrock.features8.

4. "Reeling in the Years," March 25, 1978, *Hot Press*, http://www.hotpress.com/archive/549300.html.

5. Clayton-Lea, *U2 Popaganda*, 228–29.

6. "Reeling in the Years," *Hot Press*, March 25, 1978, http://www.hotpress.com/archive/549300.html.

7. Clayton-Lea, *U2 Popaganda*, 231.

Chapter 3

LIKE A STAR: REACHING HIGHER (1980–1983)

The past three years had shot past in the blink of an eye. It seemed like just yesterday that Bono had been torn between drama and music, that he was singing in front of the mirror or a crowd of a thousand. Now his voice was a regular fixture on local radio and he was earning a reputation as the best front man in the country. He had worked very hard to learn his trade and to fit into the mold of a savvy artist with something important to say to his generation.

U2 had also evolved from Eagles covers to original songs that could move an audience and get recommended on the radio. They had learned some hard lessons and invested a lot of money and time to get what they wanted. Adam had developed into a solid bass player; Larry, who could always keep a steady beat, was now experimenting with varied rhythms; and Edge was on his way to becoming one of his generation's most distinctive stylists.

The band had some plans for their first album, and after some discussions they reached a consensus on the producer they wanted for it: Martin Hannett. He was the mastermind behind Joy Division, the most influential and important band since the Sex Pistols. Joy Division took their name from the Nazis, and their music was often just as bleak and nihilistic as the Nazi legacy. Lead singer Ian Curtis had a reputation as a lyricist of note and had one of the most distinctive voices around. Complementing his vocals were the production values that Hannett had employed to give the Joy Division records a haunting sound.

After U2 made overtures about wanting Hannett, they were invited to a recording session near Manchester, England, to observe him at work. Bono was impressed with the precision of Joy Division's studio performances. They had more experience than U2 and it showed. He got some insight into what a good producer could do to a band's sound and realized that U2 needed someone as distinctive as Hannett. Edge wasn't as impressed and thought the band was too mannered and stiff. He wanted more spontaneity and passion inside the studio, but he was aware that different personalities could discover unique approaches to the same goal.

When they had time alone with Hannett, they played him their demo for "11 O'Clock Tick Tock." He liked the song but thought the production was flat. He agreed he had something to add to the mix and he genuinely liked the Irishmen. Arrangements were made for Hannett to go to Dublin in April during Easter to record the song again. They met at Windmill Lane Studios and soon ran into difficulties. Bono got along with Hannett and appreciated his approach, but Adam and Larry came in for some criticism. Edge was also a bit surprised about the lack of overdubs Hannett suggested. Hannett was used to working his magic after the band had recorded their separate parts and never relied on overdubs much with Joy Division. U2 was a novice band and they had had problems with other producers, so they tried their best to accommodate the famed Mancunian.

The final result turned out to be a stunner. The template for U2's distinctive sound was laid with this single, and Bono was convinced of his band's uniqueness. He had taken the title from a note that friend Gavin Friday had posted on his door. It referred to the imminent end of the day and had ominous overtones that appealed to Bono's sense of drama. He wrote the lyric after U2 backed up psychobilly band the Cramps.

"11 O'Clock Tick Tock" was released on May 23, 1980, just a few days after Joy Division's lead singer Ian Curtis committed suicide. U2 had been making plans to record their debut with Hannett, but

Curtis's suicide changed everything, and Hannett pulled out over his commitments to Joy Division. Bono was disappointed but the rest of the band was relieved. They were confident that they could maintain the gains they had just made with another producer. Paul mentioned Steve Lillywhite, a producer who had recently worked on Peter Gabriel's third album and had experience working with XTC and Siouxsie and the Banshees, bands U2 admired. Lillywhite was invited to Dublin to record another demo, "A Day Without Me" and he hit it off with everyone in the band. He seemed to understand the whole band better than Hannett and was willing to work with their strengths and develop a sound in collaboration with everyone.

After the single was released in August, it was instantly recognizable and conveyed a unique "U2 sound" with Edge's echo guitar. Shortly after, U2 went to work with Lillywhite on their debut album. Lillywhite brought a fresh approach and was willing to look at idiosyncratic ways to achieve a special sound. He broke bottles, used spoons on bicycle spokes, and made Larry play his drums under a stairwell outside the studio to get a bigger sound. It was all done in fun and in a spirit of adventure, and Bono responded in kind during recording sessions. He would close his eyes and let himself go, often knocking off his headphones in an attempt to grapple with a song's particular mood. In the early days, he would often write his lyrics spontaneously whenever the feeling seemed right. He wasn't entirely committed to one version and would sometimes change a word or rewrite an entire verse. The recording process presented a different challenge, one of permanence that daunted Bono. His words mattered and as soon as they were committed to tape they would live on in perpetuity. He was having a hard time finishing the lyrics for songs and his vocals kept being pushed aside to be recorded later. Eventually, the day of reckoning came and he found himself stumbling on a general theme that tied some of the songs together—one of innocence and boyhood.

He had always recognized the importance of the naive, innocent observer as a catalyst for creativity and change. His time with Lypton Village had helped preserve and celebrate this perspective. Perhaps it was the death of his mother at a relatively early age that made him long to retain a connection to his youth. He recalled, "I had a sense that this was subject matter no one else in rock and roll had ever explored—the end of adolescent angst, the elusiveness of being male, the sexuality, spirituality, friendship."[1]

All summer the band labored on the album and expanded the concept Bono had helped define. He was also thinking visually and he had an image in mind for the album sleeve and asked Guggi's younger brother, Peter, to pose for it. It turned out to be an iconic shot that captured the innocence and vulnerability Bono was envisioning while writing the material. The final album didn't disappoint. The production was top caliber, the musicianship meshed well together, and Bono's lyrics were provocatively alluring. Comparisons were favorably made to the Gang of Four's *Entertainment!* and PiL's debut, both widely regarded as seminal post-punk albums.

When *Boy* appeared in October 1980, Ian Curtis had been dead for almost half a year and the U.K. charts were full of new-wave bands like the Pretenders, Police, and Bowie's album *Scary Monsters*. U2 began another tour of England, and their sound was a perfect clarion for the times—it bridged the underground with the mainstream and conveyed a promise for the future. Edge's guitar playing avoided familiar blues clichés and power chords for more evocative and ambiguous half-tones that reflected the uncertainty of the times. Ronald Reagan would win the U.S. presidential election in November and Margaret Thatcher had been in power for over a year already and was implementing conservative reforms Britain had never seen before. The Cold War was as frosty as it ever had been and the possibility of a nuclear war was being openly discussed.

In this gray uncertainty, U2's music offered a ray of hope. The band was greeted well in England, and Gavin Martin from the *New Music Express* noted, "Only a blind man and the dead could ignore the passion and charisma generated by singer Bono. The very essence which underpins the performance is an electric vibrancy between the stage and the dancefloor. It's something loads of groups try for, but only a few can achieve."[2]

While in England, Bono wrote a letter to his father:

The band [members] are getting tighter and tighter. The nights at [London nightclub] Marquee are very successful. Each Monday the crowd gets bigger and bigger. . . . We did three encores last week. The single sold a thousand copies and for the first time we are getting daytime radio play on Radio One. . . .

Paul McGuiness is in America at the moment planning our moves over there. We now have a rough schedule of what we're doing for the next year. . . .

So as you can see, what was once a dream is now very real. But understand that underneath there is a lot of hard work ahead, and I hope a lot of fun.[3]

After the five-week tour, U2 went on their first European tour in Belgium, the Netherlands, and France. Paul could see how the band had developed and were ready to take their music to the next level. He had dreamed of managing a successful band and knew that the key to success lay west across the ocean in the United States. That's where the Who and Led Zeppelin had made it big and it was where the Police were currently trying to break into.

In December, Paul organized a brief two-week, eight-concert tour of the eastern United States. On December 4, 1980, U2 landed at JFK Airport in New York City. It was Bono's first time in the United States and he was thrilled to be walking down the same hallowed streets as Bob Dylan, Lou Reed, and the Ramones. Two days later, on December 6, U2 played their first-ever American concert at the Ritz. Later, Bono addressed the crowd at the Malibu Nightclub: "We're not just another band from England come over here for a short time. We are from Ireland, and we're here because we want to be here, and we're spending a lot of time in your country."[4]

Then, in the middle of the excitement, John Lennon was gunned down by a crazed fan in front of his Dakota apartment building with Yoko Ono looking on. Suddenly, the mood that had been festive in the weeks before Christmas turned dark and bitter. Across the United States and the rest of the world, radio stations started playing Beatles' and Lennon's songs all day long, television stations ran specials, and newspapers were filled with feature stories. Lennon was only 40 years old and with the rest of the Beatles, he had helped carry the dreams of an entire generation with him.

Bono had always admired Lennon, particularly his eccentric, dark sense of humor, his mood swings, and his conflicted messages of violence and love. Bono also identified with the sorrow the ex-Beatle had confessed to feeling about his late mother, Julia, and recognized a kindred spirit in some of Lennon's lyrics. Lennon was above all else a courageous soul warrior who strived to be a truth teller. Bono wanted to aspire to the same in his own art, to put it in the service of something larger than himself. During the tour, he inadvertently began a tradition by adding a line or a verse here and there to one of U2's original songs. It started with "Electric Co." and in Boston's Paradise Theater he slipped in Lennon's "Give Peace a Chance" and the crowd reacted with wild approval.[5] Bono would continue to do this with other songs, virtually anticipating the mashing craze that was to follow a few years later to become one of the modern musical era's most defining characteristics.

Lennon's death also grounded U2 and Bono by reminding them of rock's roots and about their own debt to such bands as the Beatles and the Stones. Bono was too smart to be pigeon-holed into rejecting the past, as some newer bands such as Echo and the Bunnymen were advocating. Bono loved the Clash as equally as he loved the Beatles and Lennon's death made him publicly realize that fact. His stage presence took on an authority as he summoned the spirit of Lennon and others each night.

After the successful stint along the eastern U.S. seaboard, U2 returned home for Christmas. Bono was still buzzing from the experience, and he was displaying a new level of confidence. Some felt it was arrogance. He wrestled constantly with people's wrong impressions and judgments. It was frustrating for him because he too hated people who were arrogant. He saw it all the time in the bands that U2 had opened for such as the Stranglers, and he knew it was a mask for insecurity and fear. Bono was simply enthusiastic and confident in his chosen pursuit. As a Christian, he strove to be humble. In a letter to his father, Bono wrote,

> You should be aware that at the moment three of the group are committed Christians. That means offering each day up to God, meeting in the morning for prayers, readings, and letting God work in our lives. This gives us strength and a joy that does not depend on drink or drugs. This strength will, I believe, be the

quality that will take us to the top of the music business. I hope our lives will be a testament to the people who follow us, and to the music business. . . . It is our ambition to make more than good music.

I know that you must find this a ludicrous ambition, but compared to the task of getting ourselves from where we were to where we are, the rest is easy.[6]

During this break Bono, Edge, and Larry decided to take a step further in their commitment to Christianity. The tours around England, Europe, and the United States had opened their eyes to the sex, drugs, and rock-and-roll lifestyle on the road and they came together to discuss how their spirituality could help them navigate through these temptations. Adam was the only one who had absolutely no interest in any organized religion and he stayed away from these gatherings. He was even enjoying some of the so-called temptations of the road. The other three, led by Bono, traveled to Worcester, England, to attend a weekend retreat with other Christian musicians. Bono and Edge were asked to give a presentation about their faith and they referred to Isaiah 40:3 and Psalm 40 as particularly relevant for them.

The next month U2 got their first mention in *Rolling Stone* when James Henke traveled to the United Kingdom to interview the band. Bono said, "I don't mean to sound arrogant, but even at this stage, I do feel that we are meant to be one of the great groups. There's a certain spark, a certain chemistry, that was special about the Stones, the Who and the Beatles, and I think it's also special about U2."[7]

Bono was learning how to swagger for the media and punch above his weight, and it was paying off. He was getting the attention he craved and more ink was being spilt on the band. He quickly developed a reputation for being a great interview and for befriending journalists. Bono had always been able to walk into a room and quickly determine where the energy sources were, who were the people who he shared something in common with, and who might provide some assistance. He wasn't cold and calculating; just the opposite. He was genuine and warm and inspired loyalty and friendship.

The *Rolling Stone* interview was followed by a review of *Boy*, which was favorable. This was in the days before the magazine used

Bono, 21, also known as Paul David Hewson, is shown during an interview in Los Angeles, California, May 26, 1981. (AP Photo/Wally Fong)

a star system to rate albums and *Boy* was later awarded a 3.5/5 rating. The groundwork was being laid for taking on America and the plan was working with the positive coverage that U2 was attracting. The band then received some feedback regarding the cover of *Boy*. It was thought that the photograph of Peter was too suggestive of child pornography and in the U.S. context it could be misinterpreted as pedophilia. *Boy*'s cover was changed for American consumption and replaced with distorted images of the four band members. Bono was learning how different the two cultures of Europe and the United States were. Ireland was a far more religious country, but the United States appeared to be more uptight when it came to certain issues. It was an eye-opening experience that taught him that the United States was anything but a monolithic nation, and that what was happening in the area between New York City and Los Angeles was often quite different. If one could understand those nuances, one would have a better chance to succeed.

In March 1981, they embarked on a seven-week cross-country tour opening in the capital, Washington, D.C. The *Washington Post* wrote, "U2 brought to their performance a sense of refinement that has been lacking in rock for some time. U2, like the Police and the Clash, are taking new wave to the next, higher musical level."[8]

Over the course of the tour, Bono impressed record label representatives and radio DJs with his openness and willingness to chat and cooperate with them. He appeared as naturally gregarious and his approach was appreciated. He was quoted frequently and U2 got much-needed publicity. This attitude helped open doors for the band and would later work to their benefit in numerous ways that would help them get ahead. They were able to differentiate themselves from other bands, mainly due to Bono's charm, by seeming to be grateful to be playing in America. Other new English bands at the time such as PiL or Echo and Bunnymen feigned disgust or boredom in interviews, thinking it was cool to do so. It eventually became such a common pose that all these bands blended in and none stood out from the pack. U2's music was one thing, but their fresh and warm attitude was equally as important.

U.S. radio at this time was floundering and lacked the ability to capitalize on the new sounds coming from Britain and Ireland. DJs and programmers were still suspicious after the rawness of punk had turned off so many with explicit lyrics and violent imagery. They felt it was too much for mass consumption, so they resisted and avoided what they weren't certain of. Bono and U2 were transparent in their intentions and were able to allay fears, but overall the mood was conservative and the stations were relying on classic dinosaurs of yesteryear like Led Zeppelin and the Eagles to fuel airplay.

At a concert in Portland, Bono misplaced his lyric book that he had been working on for the next album. He originally thought it was stolen, but then learned that he had left it behind backstage. It had already been six months since the making of *Boy* and it was time to get back to the studio and begin work on their second album. Before formally settling in, U2 traveled to the Caribbean at the end of April for a break and an opportunity to record a new single with Steve Lillywhite. "Fire" was released later in the summer and charted poorly.

During the tour, Bono had been frequently asked for his opinion about the troubles in Northern Ireland or about Margaret Thatcher, and he hadn't really developed much of an informed opinion. He tried to answer the questions as honestly as possible: "As a lyric writer, I'm more interested in people than politics and more interested in why people should want to hit each other over the head with a broken bottle rather than where they do it . . . it being Northern Ireland. Everybody is violent, I feel."[9]

After touring in the United States, U2 went to Europe and Bono had a chance to meet two of his heroes—Bruce Springsteen and Pete Townsend. He admired Springsteen's lyrical prowess and embodiment of American values. Bono was reminded of rock and roll's roots and considered Springsteen's work a bridge between the classic rock of the 1960s and the punk ethos of the 1970s. Now, in the early 1980s, Springsteen was searching for a new sound and he was attracted to U2 and their inspiring message. U2 had felt they had something in common with Townsend and the Who. They were both four-piece bands with charismatic lead singers and a distinctive sound. It signaled to Bono that U2 was on the threshold of something huge if they could maintain the momentum with their next album.

In the summer of 1981, they entered Windmill Lane Studios once again with Steve Lillywhite and picked up where they had left off with *Boy*. The touring had solidified their musicianship and they were much tighter and confident than a year before. Larry was freely adding more varied rhythms and color while Adam filled in a deeper bottom end. They worked closely to create a solid foundation for Edge and Bono to take off. Edge was also using more effects and exploring different chord patterns in his songs. Bono was excited but since he had lost all his lyrics he was having a hard time putting together words and the pressure was piling up. Bono resorted to the Bible for ready-made themes and images and many of the songs on the second album have a sketchy feel as though they're not quite as fully developed as those on *Boy*.

As they were working, Bono was following the headlines more than ever. The touring and travel had opened his eyes to the realities of the world and stirred his interest in global affairs. As 1981 marched on, it appeared as though the Cold War was frosting over to an even deeper chill as the rhetoric between the East and West intensified. During the spring, IRA volunteer and member of the U.K. Parliament Bobby

Sands died in the Maze Prison in Northern Ireland while on a hunger strike. The protests and Sands's death attracted international attention, and Bono was pressed to answer countless questions about where he and the band stood on the issue. Growing up in Dublin was to live in a different country than Northern Ireland and Bono had never felt attached to "the troubles," as the conflict was known. But now he understood that the rest of the world had difficulty differentiating between the two sides and he was pulled into the conflict whether he wanted to be there or not. As he learned more, he realized how important and complicated it truly was and he felt ashamed about his ignorance. In response to these feelings, he wrote the haunting ballad, "Tomorrow." He wanted the arrangement to have a different feel, almost like a folk song, and uilleann pipes were added. It was a brilliant move and it gave U2 a broader palette from which to work.

Bono suggested *October* as the title for the album and the rest of the band agreed. For Bono, October was a stark month and a period of transition toward a bleak and cold winter. He felt that the international situation was going through a similar period and that things would likely get worse before getting better. The songs were also taking on a much more religious tone. "Gloria" and "With a Shout" explicitly referred to biblical scripture and "Tomorrow" overtly evoked Christ: "Come back, heal me / Jesus, come back."

In "Rejoice" Bono admitted his own limitations, "I can't change the world / But I can change the world in me," while expressing the determination to challenge himself that would continue to drive him throughout his life. Adam was becoming particularly uncomfortable with what he viewed as preachy proclamations. He wasn't a devout Christian by any means and a rift was beginning to develop between him and the rest of the group. Bono, however, felt the lyrics were ambiguous enough to be read on more than one level:

> The lyrics are like a puzzle because, on *October*, I didn't know what I was saying a lot of the time. Things came out of me on that record that I wasn't even aware were in there. People accuse me of not being specific enough in the lyrics and that is fair criticism, but I think there is more power in imagery because it can do more things—people can react on more levels.[10]

The band didn't have a decent rehearsal space yet and they had to return to Mount Temple to ask the music teacher to lend them some space for a small fee. They also agreed to play a gig backing Thin Lizzy at Slane Castle. They took the chance to perform the new material for the first time, but they bombed. The chemistry wasn't there and the new songs weren't gelling. The band lacked familiarity with the tunes and appeared as generally unsure. They needed some positive feedback, so they performed the following week in front of a more sympathetic crowd at the Greenbelt Christian Music and Art Festival in England. Bono believed that he had received a message from God to play, and he was becoming increasingly devout over the summer and during the recording of *October*.

The rapid changes in his life made Bono feel uncertain and threatened his comfort zone. He was reacting by clinging more tightly to religion. The conflict with Adam would eventually come to a head in the coming months.

When *October* was released in October 1981, it was greeted with mixed reviews and eventually failed to break into the U.K. Top 10, reaching number 11. It also failed to match the sales of *Boy* and this added to the uncertainty the band was feeling during the summer. Their old friend from Mount Temple, Neil McCormick, made an astute observation in *Hot Press* concerning the religious overtones of the songs: "It is a Christian LP that avoids all the pedantic puritanism associated with most Christian rock, avoids the old world emotional fascism of organized religion and the crusading preaching of someone like born-again Bob Dylan."[11]

McCormick's synopsis was accurate. Bono wasn't seeking to use U2 to proselytize or spread the Gospel with the objective to convert anyone; he was simply expressing his own struggle to reconcile Christian moral precepts with living the life of a rocker.

In the immediate aftermath of *October*'s release, the band arranged to film a video of "Gloria" in front of a small crowd on a barge afloat on Dublin's River Liffey. Videos were becoming more common at this time and U2 had actually recorded one for "I Will Follow" the previous year. But without a platform like a TV channel to play them, the videos disappeared. All that changed when MTV was launched in August 1981 and the video for "Gloria" happened to be in the right place at the right time. It got heavy rotation and helped establish a presence for U2 above and beyond their other U.K. peers.

U2 hit the road immediately, touring the United Kingdom and Europe while plans were being made for a U.S. tour in November and December. Bono didn't have a chance to catch his breath; he had gone from the stress of writing the material for *October* to the endless cycles of interviews and promos. Now it was time for another batch of tours that would take the band away from home for months.

After returning from Europe, the band confronted the lingering problem of Christianity's role in their lives and music. Larry decided to quit Shalom, feeling that he didn't need the pressure to do God's work, while Edge took the opposite tack. He quit U2. He wasn't convinced that the band was good enough to provide a platform for living a Christian life, so he decided to stop before he got in any deeper. When Bono heard, he was initially shocked but began to understand and admire Edge's radical decision. These were the types of choices that changed lives and he couldn't disagree that the rock world and the spiritual world that Shalom had been professing appeared irreconcilable. He too decided to throw in his lot with Edge and they both quit.

The band met with Paul and he was furious, appalled with what he considered to be a cowardly and irresponsible decision. He first pointed out the business commitments that still had to be fulfilled and then suggested that Bono and Edge were foolish to believe that they could be more effective doing God's work alone, rather than with a popular and successful band. If they were honest, they would have to muster the courage to make the harder commitment of staying with the band while also remaining devout Christians; only then could they reach out to millions of people. Paul was older and had more experience than Bono, and he had always respected his manager's opinion. Now Bono was hearing exactly what he truly believed—that being in U2 was his calling, it was what God had wanted for him all along. If not, why hadn't something else come along? God had made him the way he was, and if he was to deny it he would be turning away from God: "I couldn't let go of my faith. But what's more interesting is that don't think God will let go of me. I love it when people on bar stools rub their chins and say, 'Do you believe in God?' That's presumptuous. A much more important question is, 'Does God believe in us?'"[12]

He changed his mind and Edge quickly followed. Adam was relieved and felt reassured that the band's musical trajectory would shift away from an explicit Christian message and he credited Paul with turning things around.

The time came for the band to return to the United States and they embarked on a five-week tour beginning in November. Tensions were rising as *October* wasn't gathering momentum or the singles the band had hoped for. Bono was also frustrated that the band still seemed to be struggling at times with their skills. His own voice was being tested, and he noticed it was taking longer to recover between shows than before. At a gig in New Haven, the band got into a fight on stage when Bono went after Larry and pushed his drums toward the audience. Edge stepped in and ended up punching Bono in the eye: "Edge smacked me. It was actually a full-on rumble with all members of the band whacking at me and me whacking at them. I was pure pantomime. . . . But Edge packs a punch. There's a lesson here: never pick a fight with a man who earns his living from hand to eye co-ordination."[13]

During this tour they got more of a taste of the diversity of America outside the major cities of New York and Los Angeles. The area in between required just as much attention if U2 was to sell enough records, but it was much harder to draw a crowd than on the coasts. Bono also saw how audiences reacted to songs differently depending on where they were playing. He remembered the Sex Pistols' final tour of the United States kicking off in Texas where the band was almost physically assaulted, yet they had been the toast of the town in New York.

During the Christmas break, U2 recorded two new songs, "A Celebration" and "Trash, Trampoline and the Party Girl." A video was filmed at Dublin's Kilmainham Jail, where the 1916 uprising for Irish independence had taken place. It was an attempt at a hit single before they were to return to the United States, but the song failed to break the Top 20.

The second leg of their U.S. tour started in February, and they began to relax into their performances. Bono was feeling more comfortable on stage, and the band was also becoming more familiar with the material. They were seeing regular faces more frequently and meeting interesting people everyday. While Bono was resting from a set in New Orleans, he struck up a conversation with a young man from the Netherlands. His name was Anton Corbijn and he was a photographer who had some experience working with Joy Division and PiL. The two hit it off and agreed to work together, perhaps for the next album scheduled to be recorded later in the year.

U2 was invited by Peter Wolf of the J. Geils Band to open on a tour of arenas. It was a great opportunity for them, but Bono thought Peter Wolf was a bit old and his music too commercial for U2. He soon changed his mind after Paul explained what a great chance it would be for the band to gain precious experience and reach the next level. Who cared if contemporaries like Echo and the Bunnymen would mock them? U2 had bigger ambitions. The tour also provided Bono with another chance to observe a seasoned showman, Peter Wolf, at work. Wolf had been around the Boston scene for years as both a performer and a DJ, and he had a passion for soul and R&B. Bono was also attracted to Wolf's charisma and gained more of an appreciation for the music. He was beginning to draw a parallel between spiritual rapture and pop's unbridled fervor.

U2 returned to Ireland at the end of March and set out to tackle their next album. Bono had mixed feelings about the previous year; while U2 had grown, it had been both a difficult and disappointing process. *October* failed to raise the band's prestige and had even dented it in the eyes of those who watched the charts. However, on a personal level, Bono felt things were progressing substantially when he considered his experience with Wolf. Still, the next album would have to deliver, he knew, and he was writing all the time and questioning much more thoroughly than he had before. U2 rented a rehearsal space in Howth, in the north of Dublin, and set out to thrash out the new material.

Bono also proposed to Ali and they set the wedding date for August 21. Both families were pleased and Bono felt ready for the plunge. He asked Adam to be his best man as a way to secure a bond between them that had frayed over the last year. He admired Adam's independence and wit, and as Ali was never as devout as Bono, Adam provided a nice balance. The couple had been together for almost five years, and their love had not wavered but had only grown stronger. Ali was independent and could handle Bono's tough schedule. She was in university studying and was looking forward to her own career regardless of what might happen to U2. After their wedding, the couple went to Jamaica for their honeymoon and stayed at Chris Blackwell's home.

When Bono returned, he joined the band for rehearsals feeling rejuvenated and inspired. While away he had been working on lyrics and ideas, and he was thrilled to find that the band too had been doing the same. Over the past year, the band had opened themselves up to countless experiences and been exposed to new ways of thinking that they never imagined existed.

While in New York the previous spring, U2 was to take part in the St. Patrick's Day Parade, but they pulled out when it was announced that Bobby Sands was to be the grand marshal. Bono had no sympathy for the British government in Northern Ireland, but he was equally disgusted with the IRA. Although he and the band had more of an affinity for the hunger strikers, U2 couldn't be seen supporting the IRA. Not only would it alienate many fans, it would also marginalize the band and limit their potential to speak about certain issues if they were seen to be too partisan. It was an internal conflict that begged to be addressed in a song.

This all came together on "Sunday Bloody Sunday," a song named after two events that involved brutal massacres. The first had taken place in 1922 in Dublin's Croke Park when more than 30 people were slaughtered; the next occurred in 1972 when 14 people were shot in Derry, Northern Ireland. Bono said, "The bitterness between those two communities is ridiculous. . . . I see in both . . . aspects of things I don't fully like. But I like to think that I'd be able to go to a Catholic church or a Protestant church."[14]

Bono and Edge pushed each other to address the violence with Edge's barbed-wire riffs evoking the pain of the events. Bono struggled to find the right response and the right message and then hit upon a central theme of the song: "I won't heed the battle call." He was framing his own response as resisting the cycle of violence and was advocating against participating in the knee-jerk impulse to blow other people up. Bono had the presence of mind to understand that true peace started with oneself: "It was only when I realized that the troubles hadn't affected me that they began to affect me. The bombs may not go off in Dublin but they're made here."[15]

Using music to address social issues was nothing new, but during the previous five years or so, it had been happening more frequently with bands like the Gang of Four and PiL going after social inequities in England. The Clash, on the other hand, had begun their career diametrically opposed to establishments in both government and the music industry. At the end of 1980, they had set their sights further afield releasing *Sandinista!*, a three-disc salvo in support of the Nicaraguan revolutionaries. Bono had also felt a kinship with Joe Strummer, and he was finally ready to step into the political ring with the new material U2 had been writing.

Bono also wanted to work again with Steve Lillywhite as the producer, and the rest of the band agreed. But when Lillywhite was contacted he refused, saying the band should try someone different, branch out, and take a few chances. They briefly considered others, most notably Sandy Pearlman, the producer responsible for the Clash's first commercial breakthrough, *Give 'Em Enough Rope* and who had worked with Blue Oyster Cult. Bono insisted on Lillywhite. He felt comfortable with him and was aware that the next album had to take U2 to the next level. He couldn't help feeling as though *October* was a missed opportunity and that he personally had not performed as well as he could have. Lillywhite finally agreed, and the band started recording during the summer at Windmill Lane Studios.

Together with "Sunday Bloody Sunday," U2 was also writing other songs addressing contemporary political issues. "Seconds" was U2's statement on the Cold War. When Lillywhite heard the band playing it, he encouraged them to consider looping in an old chant from *Soldier Girls*, a documentary by the filmmaker Nick Broomfield. Bono loved the idea and the rest of the band was happy with the end result. It became one of the decade's earliest attempts at sampling.

As with *October*, the band also wanted to use acoustic instruments in new and unusual contexts to convey their Irish heritage. Edge met violinist Steve Wickham one day at a bus stop and invited him to the studio for a session. Wickham, who would later go on to find fame with the Waterboys, ended up playing on two tracks, "Sunday Bloody Sunday" and "Drowning Man." His contribution was significant and his riffs elevated the songs and put a stamp of tradition on an otherwise modern production. The songs also sounded otherworldly, new and old at the same time, and they furthered the development of U2's unique sound. No other band on the scene in 1982–1983 was coming close to this juxtaposition of punk and folk.

Bono's lyrics were more sophisticated and subtle and refrained from overt declarations of Christianity. Rather, Bono conveyed the desperation of a man whose faith was slipping away in the metaphor of a drowning man in the song of the same title; and in "Surrender" the references to war and a city under siege also referenced the Christian ideal of surrendering the soul to forces greater than oneself. On "New Year's Day," Bono addressed the struggle of the Polish Solidarity Union against totalitarianism, while simultaneously referring to the resurrection: "I will begin again."

But in one of the most blatantly Christian songs U2 had ever recorded, "40," the music transcends the message and it's transformed into a secular gospel that eventually appealed to a huge swath of listeners. The song "40" also pointed the way forward for the band, suggesting that they could be melodic and soulful, while still retaining a primordial punk intensity. Bono took the lyrics directly from the Bible's Psalm 40:

I waited patiently for the LORD; and he inclined unto me, and heard my cry.

He brought me up also out of an horrible pit, out of the miry clay, and set my feet upon a rock, and established my goings.

And he hath put a new song in my mouth, even praise unto our God: many shall see it, and fear, and shall trust in the LORD.

Edge contributed a loquacious bass line beneath the hymnlike vocals while Adam was out of the studio. The final song recorded on the album, "40" included the perfect refrain to question their fans and contemporaries: "How long to sing this song?"

Bono's feelings were confirmed in the choice of Lillywhite. The band was excelling and firing on all cylinders and exploiting their strengths. Bono wanted the album to rock harder, more intensely, and he kept pushing Edge to go all out on guitar like the Clash's Mick Jones.[16] On "Sunday Bloody Sunday," "Refugee," and "Two Hearts Beat as One," Edge's guitar attack is unhinged and full of renegade angst. Larry's playing had fully developed under Lillywhite's tutelage, and he had incorporated his own distinctive rhythms throughout. Lillywhite used his own production techniques to bring out a big percussive sound that was instantly recognizable. Larry drew on his marching band training and added military snaps on his snare that propelled the opening track and introduced U2's third album, *War*.

Before the album was officially released, U2 went on a mini-tour in December to test out the songs. They traveled to Sweden, where U2 flew to the northern city of Salen and drove to the outskirts to film the video for "New Year's Day." Bono was freezing in the minus 10-degree temperature but agreed with the vision and theme of the landscape of snow contrasting with the passion of the music. *War's* theme was a chilling warning and comment on the Cold War and the possibility of a nuclear holocaust. Bono felt the times were uncertain and didn't bode well for the future and that the perfect embodiment of the zeitgeist would be the face of a wounded, abused child—damaged innocence. It was the flip side of *Boy's* innocence, and Bono relished the dramatic contrast.

Arrangements were made to photograph Peter Rowan once again for the album cover and the results were startling. The picture of him staring out in an accusatory glare as if to say, "Look what you've done to me," was a powerful message to send. It was a radical change from what usually had been associated with U2 and it caught the attention of anyone who laid their eyes on it. It also captured the confrontational mood of the songs. Anton Corbijn, who Bono had met the previous spring, was asked to come along to Sweden and he took black-and-white photographs of the band in the snow. They looked like they were ready for battle and the photographs were at odds with the other neon colors and primped styles of the day. The album visually set U2 apart and was already making a significant impact before the music was actually heard.

U2 returned to Ireland, and while they were playing in Belfast, the epicenter of the troubles, Bono spoke to the audience before "Sunday Bloody Sunday": "This is called 'Sunday Bloody Sunday.' It's not a rebel song. It's a song of hope and a song of disgust. We're gonna play it for you here in Belfast. If you don't like it, you let us know."[17]

The crowd loved the song, and it provided Bono with the certainty he was looking for to leave it as the opener on the album. After the brief tour, the band went back to Dublin for Christmas and put some finishing touches on the album before emerging in January on *Top of the Pops* performing "New Year's Day." The song and performance helped generate a substantial buzz throughout the United Kingdom and when *War* was released on February 28, 1983, it shot to number one in the United Kingdom. Bono was emerging as the band's spokesperson and in an interview with the *NME* he revealed how engaged he was with the issues of his own era:

> You have to have hope. Rock music can be a very powerful medium and if you use that to offer something positive then it can be very uplifting. If you use your songs to convey bitterness and hate, a blackness seems to descend over everything. I don't like music unless it has a healing effect. I don't like it when people leave concerts still feeling edgy. I want people to leave our concerts feeling positive, a bit more free. Things might look very gloomy, but there is always hope. I think there is a need to develop a new political language to get over what is happening. . . . A lot of people can't handle these times and they are turning to things like heavy drug use. In the area of Dublin where I live there are 15-year-old kids using heroin. They can buy little ten-packs for £10. A lot of people just can't handle this age.[18]

Bono felt vindicated and relieved over his desire to work with Lillywhite. It had paid off and they achieved what they had been after over the past six or seven years of performing together. But they still had to conquer the United States. Before they could, they first had to complete a European tour. While in England in March, *War* knocked Michael Jackson's *Thriller* out of the number one spot. U2 was a hot commodity and they were catching on. Every day Bono was learning something new and adjusting to the limelight. Journalists and radio DJs were scrambling to talk to him and he gave "good copy," as they say in the industry. He was full of bravado and seemed fearless, but his charm undercut any semblance of conceit. Bono was prouder of *War* than anything else U2 had done to date:

> I believe that more than any other record, *War* is right for its time. It is a slap in the face against the snap, crackle and pop.

John Lennon was right about that kind of music; he called it "wallpaper music." Very pretty. Very well designed. Music to eat your breakfast to. Music can be more. Its possibilities are great. Music has changed me. It has the ability to change a generation. Look at what happened with Vietnam. Music changed a whole generation's attitudes towards war.[19]

Bono was also being taken more seriously by politicians courting the youth vote. In November 1983, he was asked by the Irish prime minister Garret Fitzgerald to serve on a national committee for unemployment. He soon became disappointed with the bureaucracy saying, "They had another language, committee-speak and it wasn't mine."[20]

U2 arrived in Paris to shoot the video for "Two Hearts Beat as One." They set up their gear at the Sacre-Couer Basilica in Montmartre and filmed the video edited with scenes of a fire breather and an acrobat. The sky is an oppressive gray and the band is dressed in leather coats and boots. Edge wears a wide-brimmed hat and Bono's hair is cut into a mullet with highlights. Larry wears his blonde hair in a punk spike and Adam's hair is bleached and cut a little shorter than it appeared on the cover of *October*. The video serves as a portrait of an unpretentious band braving the harsh elements in the shadow of history.

In April, U2 flew to the United States for a three-week tour. "New Year's Day" was getting ample radio play and was on regular rotation on MTV. The band finally had something to build on and they embraced the challenge, hitting the ground running and putting on blistering performances all over the northeast. After just a few weeks, however, Bono's voice was shot and he had to see a doctor. He was advised not to talk between shows, which was virtually impossible as he was still getting the lion's share of attention for interviews. The questions were coming more frequently about politics and social issues and with *War* he was unflinching in his answers:

Revolution starts at home, in your heart, in your refusal to compromise your beliefs and your values. I'm not interested in politics like people fighting back with sticks and stones, but in the politics of love. I think there is nothing more radical than two peoples loving each other, because it's so infrequent.[21]

Bono had been listening to a lot of John Lennon and reading about what he had to say about love and revolution. He had recognized a kindred spirit in Lennon after his mother's death and understood the pain that Lennon carried with him for much of his life. Bono admired the way Lennon spoke truth to power and his fearless pursuit of justice, even if it alienated friends or brought negative publicity. Bono wanted to follow the same tradition, but he wouldn't be as radical as to condone violence in any form. He drew the line there and could never support the IRA's position as Lennon had once done with his own song, "Sunday Bloody Sunday." Rather, he would stand firm for peace and love, even if it attracted the criticism of his peers in other bands like the Clash. He was ready to be an iconoclast and proud to stray from the herd.

Bono and the rest of the band were also doing research and listening to everything they could get their hands on. Most of this involved making up for lost time by exposing themselves to the classic bands of the 1960s such as the Velvet Underground, Stones and Bob Dylan's recordings with the Band. Bono had never really gone beyond his brother's record collection or what was on the radio, and now in the United States he was getting up to speed.

He was also continuing to insert other lyrics and verses into U2 songs. This early form of sampling was unique to U2, and Bono was regularly adding Chubby Checker's "Let's Twist Again" and "Send in the Clowns" to "The Electric Co." After hearing the sampling experiments on *Sandinista!* that the Clash had copped from rappers like the Sugarhill Gang Bono wanted to do more of the same.

In May, U2 played to their largest audience yet at the US (as in 'we') Festival when they joined the Clash and Pretenders to play to over 300,000 people. It was an exhilarating event and Bono was excited. He had been acting out on stage more so than ever before, climbing scaffolding and reaching out directly to the audience. At the US Festival he stole the show by disappearing for a moment and then appearing 100 feet above the stage waving a white flag. He then tossed it into the crowd and climbed back down. It raised eyebrows and concerns as well as cheers for his audacity and recklessness. Paul and the rest of the band were worried that he might hurt himself or someone else in the process and they tried to get him to tone it down. It was hard for Bono because he knew the audience loved it and he was genuinely moved by the music. One music journalist recalled one scene at a concert in Connecticut:

> Bono grabbed the white flag and ascended the left PA stacks. [The road manager's] eyes widened in alarm as Bono abruptly leapt across the three-foot gulf onto the balcony. . . . Bono paraded along the foot-wide balcony between astonished fans and a thirty-foot drop to the crowd below. When he knelt on the narrow ledge and began singing fans held onto him to prevent a possible fall. Bono stood up, pivoted and returned the way he had come . . . After Bono completed a jump back onto the speaker stack, [the road manager] visibly relaxed.[22]

Paul could see that the band had reached a new level and sought to film one of their live performances. He found a venue outside of Denver at Red Rocks, an outdoor amphitheater high in the Rockies. It could hold 7,000 people and Paul was confident that U2 could fill it to capacity if the promotion was done right and if the weather held out. He took a gamble and threw everything the band had into making it a reality. The show was set for June 5, but unfortunately on the morning of the gig it started to rain. For a moment Paul considered canceling but he resisted and forged ahead.

The gamble turned out to be a huge success and two hours before U2 was scheduled to take the stage the rain let up. A mist rolled in and created an otherworldly effect when coupled with the torches of the amphitheater. Red Rocks didn't sell out, but the 5,000 fans who made the journey braving the elements were true diehard supporters. Bono responded in kind and fed off the crowds' intense devotion and energy. The entire gig was captured on video and was released as *U2 at Red Rocks*. It was heralded as a gritty and raw performance in an age of studio wizardry and U2 was celebrated as the best of the new bands. MTV put *Red Rocks* on heavy rotation and, throughout the United States, Bono became associated with the imagery of the white flag and militant passion. *Rolling Stone* singled out the video's version of "Sunday Bloody Sunday" as one of its "50 Moments That Changed the History of Rock and Roll."

U2 had also received an invitation from the Chicago Peace Museum to donate to an exhibition called "Give Peace a Chance." The band gave Bono's original handwritten lyrics for "New Year's Day" and some props from the *War* tour, including the stage backdrop. When the exhibition opened in September, it included donations from Bob Dylan, Stevie Wonder, and John Lennon. The museum also included an exhibition dedicated to Martin Luther King Jr. and the civil rights movement, and another called "The Unforgettable Fire," dedicated to the Japanese survivors of the nuclear attacks in Hiroshima and Nagasaki.

The band finished off the tour at the end of June in New York City. They could now look back and see how far they had come and rest assured that they had achieved what they had set out to do. U2 was on fire and had captured everyone's attention. The band managed to occupy both niches as a new alternative group and appealing to more conservative audiences who still looked to past musical heroes for reassurance.

U2 returned to Dublin and played a few more shows over the summer with Bono still tempting fate and getting carried away on stage. The rest of the band, including Paul, finally took him aside and explained that he would have to stop. He finally agreed to tone it down.

Under a Blood Red Sky from U2's Red Rocks show was released in November as an eight-song mini-album just in time for the band to travel to Japan for the first time. They received a huge welcoming and were blown away by the adulation of the fans, as well as Japanese culture. Bono was also reading a lot about the history of World War II, the nuclear bombings, and Martin Luther King Jr. He was committed to addressing these themes in the new songs he was preparing for the next album.

NOTES

1. *U2 by U2* (New York: HarperCollins, 2006), 189.

2. Gavin Murphy, "U2: Marquee Club," November 30, 1980, www.u2tours.com: http://www.u2tours.com/displaymedia.src?ID=19801127&XID=105&Return.

3. Bill Flanagan, *U2 at the End of the World* (London: Bantam Press, 1995), 523–24.

4. David Schaffer, *Bono* (New York: Lucent Books, 2004), 6.

5. Carter Alan, *Outside Is America: U2 in the US* (Boston: Faber and Faber, 1992), 25.

6. Flanagan, *U2 at the End of the World,* 524.

7. "U2: Here Comes the Next Big Thing," *Rolling Stone,* February 19, 1981, http://rollingstone.com/news/story/7088993/u2_here_comes_the_next_big_thing.

8. Alan, *Outside Is America,* 30.

9. Ibid., 33.

10. Ibid., 36.

11. "Autumn Fire," *Hot Press,* October 10, 1981, http://www.hotpress.com/archive/549171.html.

12. Tony Clayton-Lea, *U2 Popaganda: Essential U2 Quotations* (Dublin: Hodder Headline Ireland, 2007), 26–27.

13. Ibid., 158–59.

14. Rolling Stone, *U2: The Ultimate Compendium of Interviews, Articles, Facts and Opinions* (New York: Hyperion, 1994), 14.

15. Niall Stokes, *U2: Into the Heart* (London: Carlton Books, 2005), 189.

16. "Steve Lillywhite on Producing U2's 'War," NPR, July 21, 2008, http://www.npr.org/templates/story/story.php?storyId=91380167.

17. Rolling Stone, *U2,* 14.

18. Adrian Thrills, "War & Peace," February 26, 1983, http://u2_interviews.tripod.com/index.html.

19. Rolling Stone, *U2,* 15.

20. Matt McGee, *U2: A Diary* (London: Omnibus Press, 2008), 71.

21. Rolling Stone, *U2,* 15.

22. Schaffer, *Bono,* 44.

Chapter 4

TWO HEARTS: MARRIAGE AND INTERNATIONAL FAME (1984–1987)

After the tour wound down in December, U2 counted their earnings and realized they had made a profit. They all took some time off and enjoyed some of their money, with Bono and Ali moving into a Martello tower overlooking the ocean in Bray, just outside of Dublin. The towers had been built in the 19th century during the Napoleonic Wars and some had been converted into homes. Bono was attracted to its history and to the fact that James Joyce had lived in one and had included it in *Ulysses*. He and Ali set out turning the tower into a home and settling in.

Bono worked on lyrics for the next album and was eager to continue addressing social issues involving war and peace. He knew that it was time to move on from Steve Lillywhite and look to other producers. Over the course of the last three albums, U2 had explored one dynamic with little room for variety—straight ahead exhilarating rock. Bono wanted U2 to tackle different sounds and see where it would lead. "40" had been embraced by fans as an anthemic closing number, and he was interested in blending a similar sound into other songs.

A few names came up in band meetings. Jimmy Iovine had produced *Under a Blood Red Sky* and he was interested in working more with the band. German producer Conny Plank was also considered, as was Brian Eno. At first Bono wasn't sure if Eno would be interested in lending his skills to U2, but the more he thought about it the more he liked the idea. Bono loved Eno's involvement on David Bowie's three albums recorded in Berlin: *Low, Heroes*, and *Lodger*, which Bono considered to be Bowie's crowning musical achievements. Eno had also worked with the Talking Heads and had a reputation for delivering both challenging and accessible music. He was contacted but to Bono's disappointment he declined.

Bono wasn't one to accept no for an answer, so Eno was contacted again and he finally agreed to a meeting. The band played him *Under a Blood Red Sky* and he was uninterested. Bono saw how little rock music interested Eno: "We played him *Under a Blood Red Sky*, the *Red Rocks* show, and his eyes glazed over. I now realize how awful the sight of a rock band in full flight was to Brian. But he caught something in the spirit of the band that perked his interest."[1]

When the conversation changed to process, they discovered they had some common ground. Eno spoke eloquently about creating an atmosphere where the living acoustics of the studio could be captured, and he placed a great emphasis on the interaction of the musicians. By the end of the meeting, Eno had changed his mind and was willing to give U2 a try. Bono said later: "Every great rock band in the British invasion went to art school. We never did, we went to Brian. He cata-lyzed our songwriting, allowed us to get away from the primary colours of rock into another world where we could really describe ourselves in what was going on around us. It was monumental."[2]

Eno was convinced that Bono and the rest of the band were ready to take a step outside of their comfort zone, and he was genuinely im-pressed with the bond the band shared as friends: "My first impression of U2 and my lasting impression of U2 was they were a band in a way that very few people are bands now. The music was a result of those four people, not those four instruments."[3]

While the band celebrated the decision, Island Records baulked and tried to actively discourage U2 from working with Eno. Chris Black-well was concerned that Eno would lead the band astray and break the commercial momentum U2 had accumulated over the past three years. The band's trajectory was indeed on the rise and a misstep could blunt their success and make it impossible to recover. U2 was still a relatively new band and they hadn't achieved the recognition that would allow them to take a chance with anything remotely experimental. However, Bono was adamant and was convinced Eno was right for U2. No band could grow and evolve without taking chances. He knew that was what set great bands apart from the pack and Blackwell soon backed off.

Eno had been working with a young Canadian engineer, Daniel Lanois, and part of the deal involved including him on the recording. Eno wanted someone who could handle sophisticated equipment and allow him the freedom to focus on other less detailed aspects. Bono had been using his home at the Martello tower to rehearse and he and Edge were developing some ideas. They admitted to Eno that the unique ambience of the room was an inspiration and Eno encouraged them to seek out a similar location for the entire band. Windmill Lane had been their base for the past three albums and the band was eager to find a new space.

Paul began scouting for a location, making inquiries around Dublin when he was put in touch with Lord Henry Mountcharles, the owner of Slane Castle. It was vacant and Mountcharles was interested in getting involved in the entertainment field. He had hosted concerts at Slane, including performances by U2 and Thin Lizzy the previous year. Bono loved the idea of recording at the castle and jumped at the chance. It was perfect—only an hour north of Dublin, which made it close enough for family and far enough away from the distractions of the city. In May, U2 moved in and immediately set up their gear. They noticed each room had a different sound and they experimented by placing the instruments in various locations, including Edge's guitar amp on a balcony outside.

Eno coached the band to stay with a particular riff or chord progression, letting it evolve and grow organically. He advised Bono to write spontaneously at the mic, emphasizing that the essence of emotion was integral to uncovering a song's reason for being. Eno's approach was spiritual and for him music was a sacred expression that couldn't be forced or mishandled as a product. In this way, he shared many of the same values as Bono's Christian faith, but without the religious dogma. Bono was again growing and learning that his own religious convictions needed to become unmoored from traditional standards to embrace his own reality. Music was something sacred, but he had lacked the vocabulary to articulate it. Eno helped him discover it:

> I believe the songs are already written and I think the less you get in the way of them the better. When you take up that pen, the ballpoint, or whatever it is, you start interfering with the song. I don't know if that sounds too spiritual or not, but I feel a bit like that. Like Martin Luther King, his best speeches were made when he threw away the script.[4]

Blackwell had been right that Eno wasn't interested in singles or in catering to consumer demand. He left that work to Lanois and the relationship flourished. Two early songs were identified as singles, "Pride (In the Name of Love)" and "The Unforgettable Fire," and Lanois took what Eno had developed with the band and tailored them into three- to four-minute radio singles. Eno was a master at creating sound textures like the clean arpeggios on "Bad," the refreshing synth splashes of "The Unforgettable Fire," and the murky suggestive undertones of "A Sort of Homecoming." He encouraged the band to go beyond conventional song structures and let the music be their guide.

Bono had been reading a lot of literature related to war and, in particular, the Hiroshima and Nagasaki nuclear bombings as related by survivors in the Chicago Peace Museum's exhibition, The Unforgettable Fire. This included firsthand interviews, stories, poems, and paintings. Bono drew on much of the imagery to create musical impressions and sound canvases. The title for the album could have easily referred to the American civil rights leader, Martin Luther King Jr., who was a major part of two explicit songs, "Pride" and "MLK." But for Bono, the greater theme involved the nuclear holocaust and the tension King presented to contemporary political figures like Ronald Reagan and Margaret Thatcher. Bono was fascinated by the contradictions of peace and war that seemed to be battling for the heart of the American psyche: "It's worth remembering that the Japanese are the only people on earth that really understand the voodoo of $E = mc^2$ and know what it is to have entire cities evaporated."[5]

Bono took the title for the opening song from the poet Paul Celan's maxim, "Poetry is a sort of homecoming."[6] Celan had lost his family in Auschwitz and he went on to chronicle the aftermath of the Nazi holocaust in poems like "Black Fugue," and Bono yearned to address similar cataclysmic events: "I realized that there is a battle, as I see it, between good and evil, and I think you've got to find your place in that. It may be on a factory floor, or it may be in writing songs. It may be trite looking back on it; you know, 'I can't change the world, but I can change a world in me.'"[7]

In the middle of the recording, the band moved into Windmill Lane to put the finishing touches on the album. Bob Dylan was scheduled to play a festival at Slane Castle and magazine *Hot Press* arranged for Bono to interview him. Bono was excited about meeting the legend and brushed up on his history as best as he could. But there was a small problem—apart from a few major hits, he hadn't really listened to Dylan's records attentively. He was just a casual fan who understood Dylan's historical significance and appreciated his contribution. Nevertheless, the two hit it off and Dylan engaged Bono with a conversation about Irish traditional music. Van Morrison was also there and Dylan sang all 11 verses of Brendan Behan's "The Auld Triangle." When Dylan asked Bono for a song, he had nothing to say. He was embarrassed, but became motivated to do some research into his country's tradition. Up to that point, Bono had been dabbling. After the interview, Dylan invited Bono onstage to duet on "Leopard-Skin Pillbox Hat" and then again on "Blowin' in the Wind"; but Bono forgot the lyrics and so ad-libbed the best he could.

After the concert, Bono returned to the studio to finish up the album. For the cover photo, the band opted for something completely different. Anton Corbijn joined the band touring around the Irish countryside and they found an old castle called Moydrum, near Athlone. After they got the photos, they settled on scarlet red for the main color. The script was scribbled across the front rather than being in the bold font of *War*. All the changes captured the album's gauzy atmospherics.

Rather than the bulletlike snare of "Sunday Bloody Sunday," "The Unforgettable Fire" opened with the restrained intensity of "A Sort of Homecoming." The next track was the big single, "Pride (In the Name of Love)," which managed to embody both a new sound and the old with its soaring chorus and Larry's propelling rhythm. Chrissie Hynde from the Pretenders was invited to sing backup, and Eno had coached

Bono to let himself go at the mic. The result was a passionate and emotive tribute to the album's figurehead, Martin Luther King Jr. There were some experiments such as "Elvis Presley and America." Bono allowed his stream of consciousness to dictate the shape of the melody, while Eno rewound a previous tape and layered Bono's vocals overtop. He felt the band had broken new ground on "Bad" with Eno's solid soundscape enabling him to reach for higher notes while breaking into the song's ecstatic crescendo.

The album was released in October and Bono was confident that they had accomplished what they had set out to achieve. It was a different album than anything they had recorded. He had dipped into more sophisticated lyrical territory to express the conflict he had witnessed while touring for the previous four years.

Before the album was released, U2 booked a monthlong tour of Australia and New Zealand. They had developed the habit of testing the new material by going on a brief tour before putting it out in order to sharpen its focus. Afterward, when sitting in the studio, they could listen again with fresh ears and fix anything that needed work. While Bono was in Auckland, he met Greg Carroll, a local Maori who was working as a roadie. He was gregarious and friendly and the two hit it off. He took Bono around Auckland and showed him the sights. By the end of the tour, Bono had offered Carroll a job as his personal assistant. The tour also revealed bugs that needed to be worked out. Edge had taken on the most responsibility for the new sounds and was using more effects pedals than before. It was taking some time getting used to.

Back in Europe, "Pride" was released in September with "Boomerang II," a composition Bono had written on a drum machine. They opened a European tour in France and continued on through Belgium and the Netherlands before returning to the United Kingdom. They had got in touch with Tony Visconti, the legendary producer who had worked with Bowie, T-Rex, Thin Lizzy, and more recently another Dublin band, the Boomtown Rats. He met up with U2 in Birmingham to record the band for a live album. They captured a powerful version of "Bad" and a few days later followed it up in London at Wembley Arena by recording "A Sort of Homecoming." Later in the following year, these tracks would be included on the mini-LP *Wide Awake in America*.

Around this time, the BBC ran a powerful report on a famine that had been developing in eastern Africa. It included extremely graphic and disturbing images of starving young children and the story became a central focus in the media. Bob Geldof, lead singer of the Boomtown Rats, had taken a personal interest and was in the middle of organizing a fund-raising event to benefit Ethiopia. He called Bono and caught him a bit by surprise: "I didn't know what to make of the call at first, because Bob was Irish, and we looked up to him and respected him, but all I remembered was having rows with Geldof about how he thought pop music and rock 'n' roll should stay away from politics and agitprop, be sexy, fun, mischievous."[8]

Bono later learned that Geldof was assembling a supergroup to record a song that would raise money and awareness about the plight of the famine victims. He invited U2 to London, but Bono couldn't convince the entire group to come along, so he and Adam attended the sessions. The recording was scheduled for November 25. Geldof had done a remarkable job in securing some of the biggest stars from the United Kingdom. Sting was there, as were members of Duran Duran, Spandau Ballet, and Culture Club. They came together and by the afternoon "Do They Know It's Christmas Time" was recorded. Four days later, on November 29, it was released and within days shot to the top of the charts where it stayed for five weeks. It sparked interest in the cause and raised a significant amount of money. The single also kicked off a trend of other charity singles such as USA for Africa's, "We Are the World" and Canada's contribution, "Tears Are Not Enough."

Immediately following the session, U2 flew to the United States to begin a brief tour before Christmas. Each member had made some new adjustments and was making use of new technologies. Larry was listening to a click track, Adam had started using a wireless transmitter to make it easier to move around the stage, and Edge had a battery of pedals to work with. Bono was demonstrating a more disciplined approach and wasn't taking the same reckless chances he had been taking before. Throughout the brief tour, the audiences were reacting in aggressive ways and fights were breaking out. Although the band was espousing peace and civility, their fans were preoccupied with the passion of the music. Bono was frustrated that his lyrics were not being heard or were being ignored. He had begun to use a spotlight from the front of the stage to shine on the crowd so he could see them better. It was also an attempt to calm people down and bring them into the fold, so to speak, and make them feel invested in the performance. From U2's early days, this was something Bono had aspired to, and it led to his habit of climbing above the stage and reaching into the crowd.

After returning home for Christmas, Bono reflected on the past few months with satisfaction. The gamble with Eno and *The Unforgettable Fire* had paid off and the album was being generally well received with near-universal acknowledgment that it was a bold and worthwhile departure. Radio and MTV were regularly playing their songs alongside Michael Jackson and Duran Duran, and Bono and U2 were getting known for their political and social commitment. Rumors were flying that Geldof had something else planned, maybe a huge benefit concert, and Amnesty International was expressing an interest in U2's involvement in charity work. It was a dream come true for Bono; he was part of a young successful band with integrity that was respected and being taken seriously.

Bono was rejuvenated in the company of friends and family over the holiday and he was looking forward to the following year when U2 would be spending more time in the United States. The band began rehearsing and by March 1, when the tour opened in Phoenix, they were ready. As the tour was gaining momentum, *Rolling Stone* magazine declared U2 "Band of the Eighties" and put them on their cover:

> In America . . . they have yet to notch a Top Ten album or single. Only now are they beginning to tour arena-size venues. But for a growing number of rock & roll fans U2 . . . has become the band that matters most, maybe even the only band that matters. It's no coincidence that U2 sells more T-shirts and merchandise than groups that sell twice as many records, or that four of U2's five albums are currently on Billboard's Top 200. The group has become one of the handful of artists in rock & roll history . . . that people are eager to identify themselves with. And they've done it not just with their music but with a larger message as well—by singing "Pride (In the Name of Love)" while most other groups sing about pride in an act of love.[9]

Rolling Stone had always been good to the band, giving them positive reviews and interviews from the time of *Boy's* release. U2 was a new band in the traditional mold and they appealed to *Rolling Stone*. Their music wasn't too aggressive or inaccessible and they were friendly and charming, not aloof and pretentious. Moreover, they respected the classic rock that *Rolling Stone* celebrated, as well as the boomer-generation issues of peace and civil rights.

In April, U2 sold out at New York's Madison Square Garden, and they flew over their family and friends from Ireland for the event. Ali didn't usually hang around the concerts, but she was thrilled to see Bono in such rare form taking the Big Apple by storm. It was a milestone for the band, and as Bono looked at the crowd that evening he had goose bumps. Later that month, Coretta Scott King, Martin Luther King Jr.'s widow, invited U2 to the Martin Luther King Center when they were in Atlanta. Bono invited his father, Bob, who wasn't used to attending U2 gigs. But he couldn't help but feel proud watching his once-troubled son succeed in the United States.

After the tour finished, U2 released *Wide Awake in America*, the mini-LP Tony Visconti had helped them record in the United Kingdom. They received some flak for the misrepresentation of it being recorded in America, but the eight-minute version of "Bad" became a radio hit. U2 was now being recognized as one of rock's greatest live acts, as well as producers of some of the finest studio recordings of the time. "Bad" was Bono's attempt at drawing solace from the turbulence of addiction, not just to drugs, but to anything. It addresses the one issue that haunted Bono: "If I could, through myself, set your spirit free." He regarded that effort as his life's work and music was his offering.

As they turned toward Ireland in June, Paul suggested a big homecoming concert. One was planned at Croke Park with REM and the Alarm on the same bill. They were greeted with an ecstatic welcome and all of Dublin was celebrating their success. After coming off the road, Bono usually took some time to relax and acclimatize to his surroundings and the slower pace of married life. Just as he was settling in, he received a call from Bob Geldof asking U2 to play at an upcoming charity concert in London. It was to be for the same cause Geldof had assembled Band Aid for, and the gig was to take place on July 13, less than a month away. He assured Bono that big names had committed themselves and that two shows would take place simultaneously to be broadcasted globally, in the United States and London. Bono was exhausted, but he knew it was a once-in-a-lifetime opportunity, a generation-defining event on par with Woodstock.

When he raised it with the band, he met with some resistance at first. U2 had just finished a tour and were in need of some rest. Besides, in another month they would all be rusty and could actually turn off fans. Paul pushed them to do it as well as pointing out the importance of the charity work and the need to move rock music to a higher plane, which had been U2's raison d'être since the early days. They eventually all got on board and began thinking about their set. Geldof had said that every performer was to get 20 minutes, not a second more, and U2 was scheduled to go on late in the afternoon London time, and evening in North America. They spent a few weeks nailing down "Sunday Bloody Sunday," "Bad," and "Pride." They were feeling good and Live Aid, as the event was billed, was growing in stature and size by the day. As the band prepared to leave for London, it seemed as though everyone in the rock and pop world would be performing, from Madonna to Elvis Costello and David Bowie.

Bono was feeling jittery and, along with the rest of the band, was anxious about how they would be received alongside a legend like Paul McCartney and grandiose bands like Queen. They all had their doubts. Bono then called Geldof to explain that they would need one more thing before going on the next day—a sound check. Geldof said it couldn't be done. No one was getting one. The pacing of the concert was vital to keep interest and eyeballs tuned in. If U2 got a sound check, then everyone else would demand one, and before you knew it the audience would be turning off out of boredom. Imagine a 20-minute set followed by a 20-minute sound check? Bono was relying on U2's popularity to get what they thought they deserved and in fact what they felt they needed. Geldof refused again and reassured the band it would all turn out fine. Bono didn't sleep well that night and was truly worried they would blow it.

The next day the band made their way to Wembley Stadium where 88,000 fans had gathered. They relaxed backstage, sipping wine and rubbing shoulders with David Bowie, Paul McCartney, Freddie Mercury, Duran Duran, and Chrissie Hynde while waiting for their slot to roll around. Then at 5 P.M., they began tucking in their shirts, splashing water on their faces, and preparing to take the stage just like prize fighters before a match. At 5:20 P.M., Jack Nicholson introduced U2 via satellite from JFK Stadium in Philadelphia and the band charged out on the stage to confront the biggest audience they had ever seen in their lives. Bono gave a wave and took a deep breath, absorbing the frenetic pulse of the crowd. He could see a few U2 and Irish flags in the massive throng as he tossed back his long, shaggy mullet and prepared to give his all. Larry's riff opened "Sunday Bloody Sunday" and the liftoff began.

Immediately, Bono could sense something was different about this performance. He felt giddy and was in the zone where the music and his singing had fused together as one. The onstage cameras caught him looking a bit fatigued at first, but that was soon replaced with his energetic stage presence. He grabbed a cameraman directing him to point his lens at the crowd inciting them to chant "No more! No more!" The song finished and "Bad" immediately followed. After a few words, Bono suddenly dropped his mic and began searching the front row for someone to pull onstage. This was something he had been doing during the last tour and it always won over fans. But this time the rest of the band hadn't been expecting anything because they knew they were up against a strict time limit. Bono hadn't intended to do anything either, but he had surrendered himself to the music and the thrill of the moment.

He flipped himself over the barrier and landed on a platform between the stage and the ground while audience members were reaching up to shake his hand and touch him. He pointed to a woman and gestured her to come forward. The rest of the band had completely lost sight of Bono and were anxiously playing the chords of "Bad" over and over again, hoping for his return. He finally appeared back onstage with a young woman and embraced her. Bono then picked up the mic once again and finished off "Bad," waving farewell as the band departed. What the rest of the band had missed had been caught on camera for a billion people around the world to see. It became one of the defining images of the decade and cemented U2's reputation as a band that could inspire great leaps of faith.

U2 had finished their set with a 12-minute version of "Bad" and hadn't even played their biggest hit, "Pride." The band was furious with Bono and he felt he had squandered one of their greatest opportunities. Bono returned to Ireland convinced he had delivered a failed performance. He joined Ali at her parent's home in Wexford and after a few days he got word that the press had seen U2's performance differently. Everyone was talking about Bono and U2 and raving about how Bono had embodied the spirit of Live Aid by reaching out into the crowd, breaking through the mystique that surrounded these wealthy pop stars to join forces with the wider public and celebrate their common humanity. Bono's performance was a leap of faith and it paid off. As Bono said of Bob Geldof,

> For Bob Geldof, the sight of little bits of black plastic actually saving lives was something of a shock. He had always thought of pop music as something wonderful in itself, but nothing more. I wasn't quite as taken aback by the success of it all. The '60s music that inspired me eventually helped to stop the Vietnam War, and there is no reason why contemporary music cannot have a similar importance. I've always believed that music could help to change things, not in any melodramatic way, but certainly as part of a movement of positive protest. There are new problems and we need new solutions.[10]

While U2 took a sabbatical during the rest of the summer, Amnesty International contacted Paul with an idea for a tour to raise awareness about human rights. Amnesty had begun an association with pop at the end of the seventies with the annual Secret Policemen's Ball concerts, which had helped inspire Bono, and now they were ready to take a bigger step by sponsoring a tour with some of the most popular names in music. Paul knew the band would welcome the idea and after the success of Live Aid it seemed like a natural step. He committed U2 and plans went ahead.

Meanwhile, Bono had been inspired to seek out more of a role in helping to alleviate the famine that Bob Geldof had targeted with Live Aid. He and Geldof had developed a good friendship over the past year and Bono had a huge amount of respect and admiration for what

Geldof had achieved. Band Aid, Live Aid, and the subsequent political pressure it had helped to create were crucial elements that could make pop a force to be reckoned with. Bono was looking for ways to go further with his own commitment, and over the summer he and Ali made plans to visit Ethiopia.

In September, they traveled to the village of Ajibar and stayed for five weeks at a feeding station promoting health, hygiene, and basic farming methods. Those were their official duties, but the couple also found other ways to connect with the Ethiopians by writing one-act plays and songs to sing with the village children. Bono said,

> We just went off for a month, and because we could. You know, we could afford to take the time. And kind of my life changed really there, and I saw things that you shouldn't ever see in your life. And we stayed in this—north of Ethiopia. I used to get up in the mornings. We slept in a tent. And as the mist would lift, you know, over the hills, you would see tens of thousands of people who had been walking all night to get food. They were coming to this camp.
>
> And sometimes, they would leave children there and walk away from them. And we would get to the children, and those children would be dead. And sometimes even worse things would happen, like a man came to me with his beautiful, beautiful boy, and said, "Please, here is my child, I can't look after him. Will you take my child? Because I know my child will live in your hands and not in mine."[11]

To be in the biblical land of the queen of Sheba was an awe-inspiring experience for Bono. He was writing copious notes and lyrical ideas were coming fast and easy. He had brought his camera along and was also recording his trip through a series of stunning portraits that would later become the book, *Strings of Pearls*. The trip also provided the couple with an opportunity to spend some precious time alone, away from friends and family, doing the work they felt made a real difference.

Ethiopia was also the home of former king Haile Selassie who had become an icon for Rastafarianism, the quasi-Christian sect based in Jamaica. Bob Marley was its most famous proponent and had sung

Selassie's praises and referenced biblical themes related to Ethiopia before he had died in 1980. Bono had grown fond of reggae through his association with Island Records, who had signed Marley first, and his time spent in Jamaica recording and honeymooning.

The experience came to an end and Bono had little time to reflect. He immediately got on a flight from Dublin to New York on his first day back. Little Stevie Van Zandt, who had just quit as a guitarist in Bruce Springsteen's E Street Band, had written a song protesting the apartheid regime in South Africa. It was called "Sun City" after the resort in South Africa that lured Western bands to play with lucrative payments. Queen had actually played and Van Zandt noted the hypocrisy of watching Freddie Mercury triumph at Live Aid, a benefit for Africa, while inadvertently lending his support to one of the most contemptible regimes on the continent that institutionalized racism.

All across campuses during the 1980s the antiapartheid movement had been gaining momentum and Live Aid inspired Van Zandt to form Artists United against Apartheid and record a benefit song and video. He had called on some of the premium talent for the song and video, including Bob Dylan, Miles Davis, Big Youth, Lou Reed, Keith Richards, George Clinton, and Bonnie Raitt. After they had recorded the song and video, Bono hung out with his old friend Peter Wolf and the pair went to visit the Rolling Stones who were in New York recording their album *Dirty Work* with Steve Lillywhite. They all hit it off and Bono jammed with Jagger and Richards until the early hours of the morning.

When Bono returned to his hotel room he was so excited that he stayed up writing the lyrics to a new song, "Silver and Gold." In the morning he contacted Richards and was invited to the studio. Richards and Ron Wood listened to Bono's new song and liked what they heard. It was an attempt at the blues, but with a contemporary twist. Wood added some raw slide guitar and Richards held down the rhythm with his trademark ramshackle style. When Bono played it for Van Zandt he said he had to have it on the *Sun City* EP, but the sleeves had already been printed. As a result, when the album was released it came with a sticker announcing the inclusion of "Silver and Gold" as it was too late to include it in the credits.

Bono wrapped up in New York once again feeling elated over what had transpired. Not only had he met the legendary Stones and stayed up swapping songs together, but he actually made a recording with one of their founding members, perhaps the greatest rock-and-roll guitarist of all time—Keith Richards. When he returned to Dublin, he hung low for a few months with Ali and friends before resurfacing in December to record with the traditional Irish band Clannad. Bono's interest in Ireland's traditional music, or folk music, showed up on *October*'s "Tomorrow" in the form of the uilleann pipes. Clannad had been making music for over a decade and had gained a level of respect and notoriety throughout Ireland that was unsurpassed in their field. "In a Lifetime" became a Top 10 hit, peaking at number 5 on the Irish charts.

Bono had been consciously cultivating an interest in traditional music on both sides of the Atlantic since he had met Bob Dylan the previous year. After that meeting, he began to understand that the roots of contemporary music lay in the past, in the music of his ancestors. At that time, music was performed, written, and enjoyed purely as a form of entertainment or artistry. The commercial appeal wasn't much of concern before the introduction of the phonograph. When people played or listened to traditional music, they were participating in its creation, it was an active exercise and not simply a passive one. Bono felt it spoke more directly and honestly to a person, their yearnings and joys in a way that wasn't manufactured or contrived. This was what he was after as he began listening to O'Carolan, Planxty, Hank Williams Sr. and Robert Johnson. He saw himself summoning the same spirit but using the contemporary tools of the modern studio and technology to express it.

With this in mind, U2 began rehearsing songs for their next album in early 1986 at Adam's home studio at Danesmoate in the south of Dublin. They asked the team of Brian Eno and Daniel Lanois to produce once again and they were eager to continue what they had started on *The Unforgettable Fire*. Eno had always been a huge fan of American gospel and the early rock-and-roll sounds of the doo-wop groups such as the Silhouettes or the blues of James Ray.[12] He could see that Bono and the band were on a similar journey of discovery of meshing together different traditions. It was rapturous and as Eno has said, "When the whole thing gels together you're much more and much less than you thought you would be at the same time."[13] Lanois too was a big fan of roots music, but also of technology and the potential it embodied. The vision for the next project would be a shared one.

Through the winter and into the spring of 1986, U2 kept working on ideas and developing themes. Bono was writing lyrics that drew upon images and events from his experiences in Ethiopia as well as his impressions of the United States. Edge was experimenting with guitar sounds and trying hard to avoid the old rock-and-roll clichés and power chords that relied on blues scales. While Edge respected and was a fan of such guitarists as Rory Gallagher, he felt it had been taken as far as it could be. Adam was delving into club music, heavy on bass and rhythm, while Larry was investigating Americana musicians such as Emmylou Harris and Willie Nelson. The group was at a point where they all had a similar understanding of the direction of U2's music, but they were exploring their own interests and bringing back what they found.

People were dying to know what U2 was up to and the pressure to release something or at least provide some insight into what direction they were taking was enormous. Up until that point, U2 had been averaging an album every 15 months or so, and it was now already 14 months and nothing was being announced. To address some of the speculation, at the end of January, U2 appeared on Irish TV performing three songs. It was a ramshackle and pretentious performance, but also very revealing for showing the audience where U2 was at. They had a new look that was more to do with hippies and motorcycles than synthesizers and Day-Glo technicolor. Bono referred to "Womanfish" as a song about a mermaid, and they covered Bob Dylan's "Knockin' on Heaven's Door" with Bono giving a shout out to Ronald Reagan who had been elected to a new four-year term as president the previous year. "Trip through Your Wires" was the only song that would appear on the next album over a year later.

In the wake of Live Aid, benefit concerts were springing up everywhere. Farm Aid had been initiated by comments Bob Dylan had made regarding American farmers, and fans in Ireland began asking questions about Irish problems such as the high unemployment rate. In June, "Self Aid" was organized in Dublin attracting such acts as Van Morrison, the Pogues, and Paul Brady. U2 put together a six-song set that leaned heavily on classic rock, covering Eddie Cochran's "C'mon Everybody," Dylan's "Maggie's Farm," and John Lennon's "Cold Turkey." The concert generated some criticism, suggesting that it would likely worsen the problem of unemployment because it was letting the government off the hook. The criticism got under Bono's skin and while singing "Bad" he angrily mentioned "cheap Dublin magazines" in response. U2 was getting a taste of the cliché that the Irish are like a bucket of crabs, each pulling the other down as it tries to escape. The Irish have had a habit of criticizing or viewing with suspicion those who achieve success beyond its borders. It was something Bono was aware of: "I've a funny feeling that it's the little things that I hate about Ireland that I secretly love. I probably like the hard times that they give us here. It makes a change. It definitely works against rather than for you that you're in U2. People are incredibly cynical about success."[14]

Amnesty International had successfully organized the Conspiracy of Hope tour for June and it kicked off in San Francisco with Peter Gabriel, the Police, and Bruce Springsteen, among others, participating. Running for two weeks across the United States, it generated excellent publicity for the human rights organization and recruited thousands of new members while raising over $3 million.[15] It wrapped up in New York with the finale, including the Police passing the torch to U2 to close the tour. Music journalist Bill Flanagan wrote,

> The great compromise was that U2 got off the stage in time for the Police to have a good chunk of prime television time . . . and at the finale of the Police's (excellent) set they went into "Invisible Sun," their haunting song about the troubles in Northern Ireland. One by one the members of U2 emerged from the wings and took over the Police's instruments. . . . Bono stepped up to finish singing the Police's song. It was a graceful gesture, the outgoing Biggest Band in the World publicly handing off the baton to the new one.[16]

Bono was feeling more comfortable in his role as a spokesperson and he was addressing issues from the stage and in press conferences. However, it was a sympathetic crowd, one that supported the politics. Bono said,

Something like Amnesty International isn't really about left or right, or the light and shade of political philosophy. It is about truth on a higher level. The notion that there are people in the world still being tortured on the scale of Nazi Germany is a truth that is still being generally resisted in 1987.[17]

When the tour finished, Bono returned to Dublin and then flew to Texas for the second annual Farm Aid concert. While there, tragedy struck. Greg Carroll, his personal assistant from New Zealand, was killed in a motorcycle accident in Dublin. He and Ali immediately flew to New Zealand where Greg was given a traditional Maori burial. It was a body blow for Bono who loved Greg like a brother and was responsible for elevating him to his role as personal assistant less than two years before in the run-up to the release of *The Unforgettable Fire*. As Bono was helping to lay him to rest, he promised Greg's family that his death wouldn't be in vain and that he wouldn't be forgotten.

He and Ali returned to Dublin just in time to pack for another trip, this time to Central America. Throughout the past few years President Ronald Reagan's administration had been supporting rebel groups throughout the region, including Nicaragua and El Salvador. The justification given was that the government of Nicaragua was sympathetic to the communists and provided support to the Soviet Union. The rock community had been suspicious of the U.S. intervention since the Clash released *Sandinista!* in 1980. Bono was introduced to a Christian organization through the Glide church in San Francisco, which arranged for Bono's visit to El Salvador and Nicaragua.[18] It was a particularly political move that inspired Bono: "I had an extraordinary time in Nicaragua, and fell in love with this very musical, very cultural place. The ideas of the revolution were, from my point of view, a coming together of many of my interests: Christianity, social justice, artists in power."[19]

One day, about 100 miles north of San Salvador, the capital of El Salvador, Bono, Ali, and their group came under fire from government forces while visiting rebel villages. It frightened all concerned and they later witnessed other villages that had been completely wiped out because of their support for the rebels. Both instances provided more material for lyrics and song themes. It had been a grueling and emotionally taxing few months and when Bono finally returned to Dublin he was in need of some serious downtime. He spent time with old friends Gavin and Guiggi and returned to Danesmoate with the rest of the band to further develop the new material.

In the middle of rehearsals, blues legend B. B. King's tour came through Dublin and Bono struck up a friendship that would eventually lead to them recording together in the future. Eno and Lanois joined the rehearsals and met the new engineer, Flood, who had been working with the band. He had experience with Nick Cave and the Bad Seeds and New Order and was very adept at the technology required at the sessions. Lanois had also been working with the legend Robbie Robertson from the Band, and U2 agreed to help him with some tracks on his forthcoming album.

Eno and Lanois suggested they move from Danesmoate and over to Windmill Lane Studios through the winter of 1986–1987 and, as usual, the recording was painstaking. They were feeling the pressure from the press and their fans to produce something truly exceptional. Expectations had been raised very high, and it is often the case in such situations that the only way to go is to fall. Bono was aware of this, but he was determined to live up to U2's billing as the band of the 1980s and deliver one of the greatest records of the decade. He was pushing Edge to rock out, drill down into the passion of the song without reverting to the old sturm and drang of *War*. Edge did as requested and was developing gorgeous, panoramic riffs that would elevate the melodies Bono sang.

In his personal life, ambition and drive were putting pressure on his marriage and he compared his own situation to other friends and contemporaries in an unfavorable light. He admired Shane MacGowan and was worried that his own domestic life was dulling his artistic edge.[20] These doubts led to one of U2's greatest songs, "With or Without You," which captured the conflict he was feeling. Other concerns about social justice were finding expression as well. Bono had discovered liberation theology during his trip to Central America and from his meetings with such figures as Ernesto Cardenal, a Roman Catholic priest, poet, and a minister of culture in Nicaragua, as well as Comadres, also known as the Mothers of the Disappeared, based in El Salvador. "I think the danger of liberation theology is that it can become a very 'material'

ethic, too material. But I am really inspired by it. If you're not committed to the poor, what is religion? It's a black hole."[21]

Bono's religious convictions were taking on a far more pragmatic
and, some would say, revolutionary nature. As others have pointed out,
Jesus Christ was a true radical, a revolutionary for love because he chal-
lenged the status quo and condemned leaders who engaged in violence.
Bono was becoming more convinced that the U.S. administration was
actively undermining a genuinely just society in Nicaragua and the
only reason he could see was that it was for power and profit, not for
freedom or the well-being of its citizens. He addressed these concerns
in "Bullet the Blue Sky" over a musical landscape that recalled an updated version of Jimi Hendrix and Vietnam.

Another issue that was plaguing the youth of Ireland was drug abuse,
specifically heroin addiction. Bono had seen Thin Lizzy's Phil Lynott
fall into its clutches, eventually overdosing in 1986. In his old neighborhood, he had also seen the Ballymun towers become infested with
alcohol and drug use. In "Running to Stand Still," he told the sad story
of a couple who "suffer the needle chill" and succumb to a life in death
existence. He understood that addiction went beyond drugs and could
include just about anything that a person became fixated on, including
love. In "With or Without You," Bono was putting into song the conflicting feelings he was experiencing in his married life. He knew in his
heart that Ali was the one, but the domestic trappings and day-to-day
events had been weighing on him.

"One Tree Hill" was Bono lamenting Greg's passing. The title referred to the location overlooking Auckland where Greg took Bono
when they first met. Bono was feeling more confident about his lyrics
and he had a lot of notes to work from. Challenges were arising from
the recording process and "Where the Streets Have No Name" was
causing the band a lot of grief. Lanois and Eno took to using charts and
extensive notes in an attempt to try and outline the structure of the
song. Edge was struggling to find the right balance of effects without
compromising the song's internal tension.

Paul was getting concerned with the amount of time being spent
on the album. It was now almost two years since their last one and he
knew fans and the press had very limited attention spans. U2 needed to
get some new music released soon or all the momentum they had built

up would be lost. He asked Steve Lillywhite to come in and help usher the process through. Paul was confident that Lillywhite had the ability to round things off, identify the strongest elements in an arrangement, and craft radio-friendly songs. Lanois and Eno knew textures and atmospherics, but making hits was the least of their concerns. Paul understood U2 needed both integrity and commercial appeal. When the recording was finished, Lillywhite passed the masters to his wife, Kirsty MacColl, and asked her to sequence the songs. She did and the rest of the band agreed with her decision.

For the album cover, the band was certain that they wanted an image to capture the sense of yearning and quest that were the album's main themes. Over the past two years, the pop world had changed and a nostalgia for the 1960s had arisen, fueled in part by Live Aid and other benefits. Fringe coats and long hair replaced suit jackets and tinted highlights. Bono felt as though he was living through another era where the real leaders of dissent were musicians like him who spoke directly to the corrupt leaders of their time. The location for the album had to be austere, not excessive. The desert seemed like an ideal location to explore, and the band joined Anton Corbijn in Los Angeles. They drove out to the Mojave Desert and Death Valley and spent a few days taking photos. When they got back to the studio they chose a shot that had been taken at Zabriskie Point in Death Valley. Throughout the desert, Bono noticed the trees that seemed to be everywhere. They were known as Joshua trees, named after the Old Testament prophet, and Bono thought the name was a perfect fit for the album. Bono was experiencing a love affair with the United States:

I sorta ODed on America. It still fascinates me, the good and the bad, the cultural schizophrenia towards America is a particularly Irish thing, y'know, 'cos of our relationship to it over the years. Plus as a writer you are filled with these fleeting impressions, the madness of America seeps through. I judge cities by the effect they have on me. New York—I write. Man, the words are falling off the buildings, they're in neon, in '30s rusty iron on the tops of brownstone buildings. They're the street names, in the cities and the people. You read Bukowski? Man, that's the poetry of America. I grew up with European writers and recently

I started to react strongly against that. All the T.S. Eliot school of highbrow, intellectual discipline. I need a language that's more direct. Flannery O'Connor's Wise Blood. That sort of writing and Irish writers—Behan, Kavanagh—they write words in a way that I want to write them and sing them. I feel such a freedom in all that poetry.[22]

With the cover shot done and the recording in the can, the album was finally released in March 1987 and immediately shot to number one. U2's time away had not had the detrimental effect that Paul had worried about and fans were waiting in anticipation. *The Joshua Tree* was recognized as a classic and was heralded as U2's greatest moment to date. Like the Beatles, U2 had demonstrated an ability to evolve with each album release, getting more mature and sophisticated. It was exciting for Bono as he felt he had reached a higher level of songwriting, one that approached poetry. His lyrics covered a huge swath of emo-

Bono performs at Madison Square Garden in New York, September 28, 1987. (AP Photo/ Corey Struller)

tional terrain, from personal politics to international relations, from emotional insecurity to religious conviction.

U2 departed for the United States soon after the album's release and began to do publicity and interviews. In Los Angeles, they decided to film a video for "Where the Streets Have No Name" on top of the rooftop of a liquor store with their old friend Meiert Avis. The band put on a mini-concert and actually rehearsed the song a few times before capturing it on film. A crowd began to gather below and word soon spread that it was U2. The police were eventually summoned and they were ordered to shut everything down.

When the tour kicked off on April 2 in Tempe, Arizona, the band had no idea that a political firestorm had been brewing, involving an issue close to their hearts. The governor of the state had recently repealed the holiday that had been set aside in memory of Martin Luther King Jr. and calls for a boycott were growing. Stevie Wonder, one of the instigators of King's national holiday, had already canceled shows in the state and now the question remained whether U2 would follow. The band faced a dilemma. They hadn't been made aware of the controversy before booking the dates and to cancel would send promoters and fans into fits of anger. Money would be lost, but that wasn't the biggest deal. It was their professional reputation that was also at stake. On the other hand, how could they be seen as supporting such a nefarious policy when they were the composers of "Pride," a tribute to Martin Luther King Jr.?

This was the type of conflict that caught Bono's imagination and it usually brought out the best in him. He began looking for ways to accommodate both positions. After speaking with members from the campaign to recall the governor, Bono gave an interview and condemned the governor's position. As he stepped onstage, he felt like a boxer stepping into a ring and was looking for a knockout. U2 opened with "Where the Streets Have No Name" and Bono was blown away by the audience's reaction and acknowledgment of the new material. Then after a few numbers, he felt his voice giving away and wasn't able to stretch it as much as he was used to. He had it treated soon after and it didn't appear as a factor in the reviews of the show. The critics were unanimous in their praise of the band's undiminished intensity. However, Bono was having a hard time adjusting to his new status as a mega-celebrity:

Like, since I was 17 I've been in this band and it so happens that most of my friends are musicians or writers, what have you. Now all my identity has been wrapped up in this life, this U2 thing. Recently, I've got to thinking this isn't such a healthy thing. In all other areas I'm a total embarrassment. Socially, God, I'm a social inept. That's what makes me laugh when people ask me what it's like being a rock 'n' roll star. I'm the last person to ask. I have no understanding of that.[23]

As the tour wound its way through the United States, *The Joshua Tree* kept earning accolades and rave reviews. The album struck a nerve and articulated what many Americans had been feeling. The Reagan years had been a clash of upset expectations and contrasting narratives. On the one hand, the propaganda machine had been extolling "Morning in America," but on the other hand, the declining standard of living for the middle class told the opposite story. Overseas, the United States was the envy of the world, but there was no denying that many of its interventionist policies, both past and present, had caught up with its reputation. Suddenly, the United States was beginning to be seen as a threat and not as a friendly ally. Bono's lyrics reflected these undercurrents in wide, panoramic verses that raised hope rather than despair. U2's music was as close as pop had come to gospel music in a very long time.

As the tour continued, U2 found themselves adding more covers to their sets from the likes of Bob Dylan, Neil Young, and Johnny Cash. They had never been interested in country and western music before, but they were developing a taste for it based on its influence on rock and roll. Country music was popular in Ireland, but only among a small group of elderly folks who represented the furthest thing from cool as could be imagined. When U2 flew to Las Vegas for a boxing match, they were invited to meet the legendary crooner, "Ol' Blue Eyes," Frank Sinatra. He and Bono hit it off. The band was absorbing as much American culture as they could and enjoying every minute of it.

Financially, the tour was a huge success. They were easily selling out 15,000-seat arenas in large cities and the media attention was reaching a fevered pitch. In April alone, both *Time* and *Newsweek* magazines included features on U2, while "With or Without You" reached the top of the charts. The tour finished at the end of May and U2 returned to Ireland before setting out for Europe. The Irish press began displaying a more skeptical view of the band, questioning their commitment to social issues and sincerity when they were making millions of dollars. Touring has always taken its toll on Bono's relationship with Ali: "My life is just a mess. When I am away, I'm not at home. When I'm home, I'm not at home. I come in when she is going out. She will not be worn like a brooch. We have a stormy relationship because she is her own woman."[24]

Despite the somewhat rude homecoming, U2 was warmly welcomed all over Europe and was succeeding in winning over each country, concert by concert. In June, "I Still Haven't Found What I'm Looking For" reached number one. Bono was still exploring American roots music and Roy Orbison became a particular obsession. The "Big O," as he was known, was enjoying renewed success and recognition from a new generation of musicians. One of his classic songs, "In Dreams," had also featured prominently in David Lynch's film *Blue Velvet*. Bono had become attuned to lead singers and was enjoying discovering the subtle differences between them and comparing himself, usually unfavorably. He finally got a chance to meet Orbison in London and they arranged to work together in the coming months. Bono had begun to write a song for Orbison, which he eventually recorded as "She's a Mystery to Me."

The band took a much-needed break in August, and Bono snatched a chance to visit the Greenbelt Christian Festival with Ali. The festival had become a personal favorite because it wasn't just about biblical prophesy, but it attracted other like-minded individuals such as Canadian singer-songwriter Bruce Cockburn who viewed the gospel as a way to promote social change. One of Bono's favorite lines from the Bible was from Matthew 6:10: "On earth as it is in heaven," which he understood as a challenge to make the world a better place.

In September, U2 returned to the United States but were booked into 50,000-seat stadium venues. Their popularity had exploded and they were now a phenomenon. Paul was eager to capture this moment on film but wanted to try and do more than just a simple concert performance. He explained his feelings to the band and they agreed to try making a feature-length film based on the tour. They budgeted enough money and then sent the word out to find a director. Phil Joanou was a 27-year-old who had apprenticed with Stephen Spielberg, but didn't have much other experience. When the band met with him they quickly hit it off and he was tapped to be the film's director.

Joanou assembled a crew and began filming immediately. U2 was now a potent force, and along with album sales they were also recruiting members for Amnesty International and allowing them to set up booths at their concerts. Just after the tour began, Bono slipped onstage at Washington, D.C.'s RFK Stadium and dislocated his shoulder. He had to wear a sling for almost a month. Bruce Springsteen, who was at the peak of his popularity on the strength of his blockbuster album *Born in the USA*, joined U2 in Philadelphia in front of a massive crowd of 86,000. For the east coast leg of the tour, Paul had booked a house in the Hamptons for the band to return to each evening after their gig, but it turned out to be a bad idea. They felt cooped up and removed from where the action was and it didn't fit with the regular pace of touring. They weren't on holiday and it was unnatural to try and decompress between shows in such an isolated environment.

As the tour progressed across the country, Bono began to look for ways to blow off steam and relax. Humor came naturally, but Bono was becoming the subject for jokes about taking himself too seriously. In response, he suggested U2 disguise themselves as a phony country band called the Dalton Brothers and play an opening spot before their concerts. They rehearsed a few country standards from Hank Williams Sr. and Johnny Cash, and the crowd loved it. Joanou was filming everything. When U2 reached San Francisco, they organized a free, outdoor "Save the Yuppies" concert at Herman Plaza. A Yuppie was the nickname for young urban professionals, who had become an influential and conservative demographic across the United States, throwing their support behind the Reagan administration. U2 opened with Bob Dylan's "All along the Watchtower," which Bono had just learned the words to before taking the stage. While performing, he spray painted "Rock N Roll Stops Traffic" on the Vallaincourt Fountain. The scene made the final cut for the upcoming film, *Rattle and Hum*, but what wasn't included was Bono's written apology to the mayor of San Francisco, Diane Feinstein.

During the recent tour, the questions about Northern Ireland diminished, but that changed on November 8, the day a bomb blew up in Enniskillen, killing 11 people. The troubles came roaring back into the headlines, and Bono felt ashamed and furious about what had happened. The night of the tragedy, he spoke onstage in Denver during "Sunday Bloody Sunday":

> Well let me tell you something! I've had enough of Irish-Americans who haven't been back to their country in twenty or thirty years come up to me and talk about the resistance; the revolution back home, and the glory of the revolution and the glory of dying for the revolution. F*** the revolution! They don't talk about the glory of killing for the revolution. What's the glory in taking a man from his bed and gunning him down in front of his wife and his children? Where's the glory in that? Where's the glory in bombing a Remembrance Day parade of old-aged pensioners, their medals taken out and polished up for the day? Where's the glory in that? To leave them dying, or crippled for life, or dead under the rubble of a revolution that the majority of the people in my country don't want.[25]

The emotions came flooding out and Bono was letting everything he had been feeling for years fly. There was never any glory in a struggle that viewed innocent bystanders as legitimate targets. Bono had seen the supporters of the IRA in the United States and had been approached numerous times by people who thought he was also sympathetic to their cause. He was anything but, and in the aftermath of the Enniskillen tragedy he had to address their misguided and depraved support.

Bob Dylan had become one of Bono's heroes ever since he met him in the days preceding the release of *The Unforgettable Fire*. Like others before, he recognized Dylan's genius and revolutionary appeal as an outsider rebel, but it was his conversion to Christianity more recently that intrigued Bono. Dylan's preaching wasn't what he admired—it was his moral vision and his lyrics. They were rooted in biblical prophecies that reflected the themes that Bono also wanted to comment on.

While in Los Angeles, he had a dream of Dylan and woke up with a song in his head. He immediately wrote the words and went back to sleep. When he found them the next morning, he wasn't sure if they were his own or belonged to Dylan. He dug up Dylan's Malibu phone number and was invited over to share it. They spent an afternoon working on "Love Rescue Me" and agreed to record together in the near future. Bono was also working on a song for B. B. King who was opening for U2 at some of their shows. After he heard the song "When Love Comes to Town," he was deeply impressed with the depth of the lyrics and was happy Bono had thought of him.

The tour continued, and when U2 found themselves in Memphis they took time out to visit Graceland, the home and final resting place of Elvis Presley. U2 then booked a session at the original Sun Studios, where legends Elvis, Little Richard, Jerry Lee Lewis, Johnny Cash, and Roy Orbison had also recorded. Bono put the finishing touches on a new song, "Angel of Harlem," written for Billie Holiday, and U2 cut the track with the famed Memphis Horns. They were slowly assembling the film footage and a soundtrack to what would eventually become their next project, *Rattle and Hum*.

The Joshua Tree tour finally wrapped up where it had started in Tempe, Arizona. U2 was now an international phenomenon that could play alongside legends like Bob Dylan, B. B. King, and Johnny Cash. Bono had become an international celebrity feted by the press and frequently asked to comment on various social issues in a way that Michael Jackson or Madonna were not. He was in the process of single-handedly transforming the image of a rock celebrity from one of luxurious debauchery to a more morally responsible and intelligent citizen of the world. The times were changing and as he returned to Dublin for a Christmas break, his mind was preoccupied with the upcoming film.

NOTES

1. *U2 by U2* (New York: HarperCollins, 2006), 148.

2. Ibid., 151.

3. "The Making of the Unforgettable Fire," YouTube, http://www.youtube.com/watch?v=W5tNDRPJZF4.

4. Ibid.

5. *U2 by U2*, 152.

6. "Quest for Fire," *Hot Press*, November 16, 1984, http://www.hot press.com/archive/549247.html.

7. Rolling Stone, *U2: The Ultimate Compendium of Interviews, Articles, Facts and Opinions* (New York: Hyperion, 1994), 35.

8. *U2 by U2*, 157.

9. David Schaffer, *Bono* (New York: Lucent Books, 2004), 48.

10. Adrian Thrills, "Cactus World View," atU2.com, March 14, 1987, http://www.atu2.com/news/cactus-world-view.html.

11. "Bono: Interview with Larry King," CNN, December 1, 2002, http://archives.cnn.com/TRANSCRIPTS/0212/01/lklw.00.html.

12. "Guest DJ Brian Eno," NPR, May 31, 2011, http://www.npr.org/2011/05/31/136723328/guest-dj-brian-eno.

13. Ibid.

14. Tony Clayton-Lea, *U2 Popaganda: Essential U2 Quotations* (Dublin: Hodder Headline Ireland, 2007), 221.

15. "Amnesty Tour: Keeping the Doors Open," atU2.com, June 22, 1986, http://www.atu2.com/news/amnesty-tour-keeping-the-doors-open.html.

16. Bill Flanagan, *U2 at the End of the World* (London: Bantam Press, 1995), 92.

17. "Cactus World View," atU2.com, March 14, 1987, http://www.atu2.com/news/cactus-world-view.html.

18. Flanagan, *U2 at the End of the World*, 96.

19. *U2 by U2*, 177.

20. Ibid., 181.

21. Rolling Stone, *U2*, 96–97.

22. "Band of Holy Joy," atU2.com, June 6, 1987, http://www.atu2.com/news/the-band-of-holy-joy.html.

23. Ibid.

24. "Band on the Run," *Time*, February 22, 2002, http://www.time.com/time/magazine/article/0,9171,212373,00.html.

25. Phil Joanou, Director, *U2: Rattle and Hum*, Paramount Pictures, 1988.

Chapter 5

BLOWN BY THE WIND: OFF COURSE (1988–1991)

Bono was invited to display his photos from Ethiopia at an exhibition in Dublin in the New Year. He was gaining recognition as a spokesperson who could speak with authority and passion on issues related to hunger and poverty. The exhibition titled "A String of Pearls" included his portraits of men, women, and children who he and Ali had met during their time in Ethiopia. U2 also spent time working on songs for the next album, which they decided would be a mix of live and studio recordings with cover songs. Joanou was still filming everything that involved the band, including jams at their new rehearsal space. They were particularly excited about a new song they had recently sketched out based on a Bo Diddley rhythm.

After kicking around Dublin for a few months, it was time to relocate to Los Angeles and finish off the new album. Jimmy Iovine, who had worked on *Under a Blood Red Sky,* was brought on board as producer and went to work, weaving the different production values together. Bono was staying at a mansion in Bel Air and settled into the L.A. lifestyle, partying frequently and hard. Soon after arriving in L.A. the band flew to New York City where the Grammy Awards were being held. U2 won their first two for Album of the Year and

Best Rock Performance for *The Joshua Tree*. U2 was up against Michael Jackson's *Bad* and Whitney Houston's *Whitney*, but it was U2 that Diana Ross announced as the winner. All four looked bewildered with joy as the camera panned over to where they were sitting. They rose from their seats, along with Brian Eno and Daniel Lanois, to receive the award. Bono stepped up to the mic and solemnly began a speech:

> It's actually really is hard carrying the weight of the world on your shoulders, and saving the whale, and organizing summits between world leaders and that sort of thing. But, we enjoy our work. And it's hard when there's fifty million people or so watching not to take the opportunity to talk about things like South Africa and what's happening there and remarkable people like Bishop Tutu and what they have to put up with.
>
> But, tonight is maybe not the night for me to do that, so instead I'd like to talk about the music, as we set out to make music, soul music. That's what U2 wanted to make. It was soul music. It's not about being black or white, or the instruments you play, or whether you use a drum machine or not. It's a decision to reveal or conceal. And without it people like Prince would be nothing more than a brilliant song-and-dance man that he is, but he's much more than that. People like Bruce Springsteen would be nothing more than a great storyteller, but he's much more than that. Um, without it, U2 would probably be getting better reviews in the *Village Voice*, but that's a joke. Sometimes they don't understand. Uh, without it, U2 certainly wouldn't be here and we are here and I wouldn't want to be anywhere else than New York City tonight. Thank you.[1]

After a night of celebrating, U2 was invited by Michael Jackson to meet with him backstage at the Madison Square Garden. Bono was excited and looking forward to seeing the legend in the flesh. But when the band discovered that Jackson had arranged for a camera crew to film the visit, they declined. Bono was uncomfortable giving up control of U2's image and the band hadn't established any understanding with Jackson about what the film would be used for.

When he returned to L.A., Bono continued working on a song for Ali, "All I Want Is You." Living on the road without her over the years had put things into perspective and he was eager to show his gratitude for her patience and love. "People have tried to figure out our marriage for years. It's simple. Relationships need management and she's a very good manager. There's still a lot I don't know about her. She's a mystery to me. Sometimes, I feel I'm not good enough for her . . . I love her."[2]

The lyrics came first and then he and Edge worked out a melody based on a simple two-chord riff. After they nailed the basics, Bono wanted to add something special to crown the song. He thought of some of his favorite songs that included orchestral codas like the Rolling Stones' "Moonlight Mile" and Elton John's "Tiny Dancer." One composer who had experience working with great artists like the Beach Boys and Tim Buckley was Van Dyke Parks. He agreed to write a coda, turning it into a throbbing six and a half minute epic tribute. U2 agreed to make it the final track on the album.

As the recording progressed, U2 felt things weren't gelling as well as they should or as they had in the past. Part of it was living in L.A. and all its distractions, but there was also something more fundamental and involved Iovine's hands-off approach to recording. He wasn't a musician and didn't feel it was his place to meddle in the songs and writing process of the band. He left them to work out their own arrangements and structures and would then be at their disposal to record the music or smooth over the sonics with production techniques. This was different from what the band was used to. They thrived on collaboration and had previously worked with mentors like Eno and Lillywhite who had built up an impressive body of work on their own and were willing to guide the band through the recording process. Without a more hands-on approach, U2 was prone to drifting and lacked the experience to create sustained and interesting arrangements.

In May, U2 returned to Dublin to get away from the mayhem of L.A. and refocus. A month later they had to be back in L.A. to finish up the album. Bono didn't like the schedule, but he was committed to finishing the album in time for an autumn release in conjunction with the film. Back in L.A., Dylan dropped by to add some inspiration, play the organ, and add vocals to a track. His duet with Bono,

"Love Rescue Me," had turned into a folk-gospel number. Bono was still targeting mainstream radio and was highly critical of its commercial agenda. When interviewed for a Woody Guthrie tribute album, he said, "There's a lie that's very popular right now, which is you can't make a difference, you can't change our world. A lot of songs on the radio perpetuate that lie for me. . . . It's the same song and it puts people in this big sleep. I think Woody Guthrie's music was much more . . . awake that that."[3]

Bono had always tried to balance the two competing elements of his profession—art and commerce. He had to walk a fine line between pandering to radio and MTV and remaining true to U2's vision of creating soul music that addressed the social issues of the time. On the one hand, he realized that the songs had to be tailored to fit a format, that hits were important to generate sales and to perpetuate U2's career. On the other hand, he also hated much of the superficiality that was involved in the getting his music heard. He didn't have much patience for bands and performers who pursued sales and image over substance. But he knew it was an ongoing battle that other bands like the Beatles had confronted without surrendering their integrity. That was how he wanted U2 to progress through the turbulence of international stardom.

As they put the finishing touches on *Rattle and Hum*, it became apparent that the album was something different from anything they had done before. Not only was it a collage of new studio recordings and live concert footage, but it also included street and church performances captured in New York's Harlem with a gospel choir. The album also staked out new territory stylistically by embracing the past in such figures as John Lennon, Bob Dylan, B. B. King, and Billie Holiday. The album was rooted in Americana, stuffed with brass horns, distorted guitar, blues, and gospel. Rather than looking forward and attempting to break new ground, it was obvious that U2 was content to explore the panoply of the American song tradition. Not everyone was satisfied with the new direction. The band was aware that the material lacked U2's typical spark and was aware of its conventionality. They had allowed themselves to become a bit lazy or complacent without someone like Eno around to question their motives or reject their attempts. But it was too late to scrap anything and deadlines were looming.

Bono was exhausted after the grueling process of recording *The Joshua Tree*, the subsequent world tour, and then the ascent to international fame. The decision to throw themselves into a huge project and film was probably made too rashly. The interval wasn't long enough to develop any new material or new themes. Bono had been used to spending his downtime exploring his inspirations, like traveling to Ethiopia or Nicaragua or reading up on Martin Luther King, Jr., and Japan's nuclear holocaust. *Rattle and Hum* became an appendage of leftover riffs and castaway themes from *The Joshua Tree*. Without the soaring production of Eno and Lanois, the project threatened to sink like a stone.

"Desire" was the first single released in early September and it shot to number three on the Billboard charts. The song revealed a more roots-orientated sound than anything on *The Joshua Tree* and was propelled by a classic Bo Diddley beat and caterwauling blues harmonica. It indicated what U2 had been busy with over the past year. The sparse video included raw footage of the band in familiar black and white, making U2 look like they were embracing a new direction that reflected the past, but not the future. The single did its job and created a buzz for the soon-to-be-released double album.

A month later in early October, *Rattle and Hum* was released with huge fanfare. A consensus soon developed that the album fell far short of *The Joshua Tree* and relied too much on half-baked ideas and structures. Bono was devastated. He thought he was involved in a tribute of sorts to the legends and musical heroes who had inspired him and so many others—people like Billie Holiday, Jimi Hendrix, and John Lennon—but critics seemed to resent the attempt. They interpreted the covers and references as an effort to align U2 with these legends. Others mentioned the issue of appropriation and felt that the blues references and the use of the Harlem choir were cheap ways to ingratiate the band into a tradition that they knew nothing about. These criticisms hurt the band, especially Bono, who had been convinced that their intentions were pure enough to transcend any shortcomings. He had been wrong for the most part.

The album's 17 songs included 8 live tracks from the previous tour and 9 new studio recordings. Two cover songs and a brief snippet came from the 1960s—"Helter Skelter," "All along the Watchtower," and

Jimi Hendrix's version of "The Star-Spangled Banner" from Woodstock. A month later Jonaou's film was released in major theaters around the world. It had a huge opening and second night but slid off the radar by the third. Critics said it portrayed the young band as too serious and self-important. Joanou had opted to make an unconventional rockumentary that bore the trademark of Martin Scorcese's classic from 1980, *Raging Bull*. Like that film, it was shot entirely in black and white with flickering shades of silver and gray illuminating certain scenes. U2 was like the boxer in the ring up onstage and every night they came to slay their own demons and put on a performance that was as liberating for the audience as it was for the band. But what was lacking was the fun and silliness that U2 employed to make life on the road bearable. Instead, there were images of Bono grandstanding and spouting huge declarations about truth and peace while calling on the ghosts of certain icons to join them in their exploits. Pompous was how it was being described and that wasn't far from the truth. U2 was experiencing a backlash and learning the hard way about how the media enjoys building up celebrities only to relish their downfall. A joke emerged: "How many members of U2 does it take to change a lightbulb? Just one: Bono holds the lightbulb and the world revolves around him."[4] The overwrought and pompous labels, however unfair, proved to be very hard to shake over the next coming years.

After the film tanked, Bono needed a break to get his mind off everything. At the end of November, he joined Adam on a cross-country road trip beginning in L.A. and continuing east to New Orleans. It was a chance for Bono to forget about the negative reviews and bond with Adam. Adam enjoyed a freer lifestyle than either Larry or Edge, which meant he indulged in a few more cocktails after everyone else had gone home or enjoyed the odd spliff once in while. Adam was also not a practicing Christian and was not as concerned about the gospel as his bandmates were. He was a secular moralist, a firm supporter of Amnesty, but he avoided referring to God in the equation, primarily because he couldn't assume to know what God would think. Bono recognized this and was becoming increasingly aware of his own shortcomings and how they were being perceived in the wake of *Rattle and Hum*. He needed a bit more Adam and a lot less God in his life.

For three weeks, they rambled like a couple of beatniks across the United States, meeting up with Johnny Cash and John Prine along the way. They chose New Orleans as a final destination and visited Daniel Lanois who had bought a house with a studio and was in the middle of recording with the Neville Brothers. The trip helped Bono put things into perspective and he realized he needed to take some extended time off to think things through before committing himself to another album. U2 still had numerous engagements over the coming year, but they hadn't scheduled any time for a new album yet. Bono wanted more time before approaching any new project. *Rattle and Hum* had taught him the problems of rushing into things and it had opened his eyes to the fickle and sometimes cruel media circus that fed on celebrities.

The band returned to Ireland for the Christmas break where Ali was three months pregnant with their first child. Edge already had two children and had struggled at times with balancing the tour schedules with family. Bono and Ali would soon be facing the same challenges and U2 would need to grow to make arrangements. Part of this required scheduling in family time as consistently as rehearsals or time in the studio. Bono was looking forward to becoming a father and felt the time was right. He and Ali had been married for five years already and family and friends had been asking when they would have children. Bono had been reluctant to commit himself until he had achieved a level of success and satisfaction where he could take a step back from U2 and place his family at the center of his life. *The Joshua Tree* had provided the fame and *Rattle and Hum* the reason to back off from the music business for some time and look to other areas of his own personal life.

After Christmas, U2 won a Grammy for Best Rock Performance with "Desire" and in May, on Bono's birthday, Ali gave birth to their first child, a daughter named Jordan. Bono was determined to be the best father he could be and he spent the rest of the spring and summer close to home. When September arrived, it was time for a new four-month tour of Australia, New Zealand, and Japan. Both the film and the album, *Rattle and Hum*, had been better received down under and U2 was looking forward to connecting with old friends and fans. In New Zealand, Bono met again with Greg Carroll's family and then flew on to Japan in late November. After receiving rave reviews and putting

on intense shows with B. B. King providing backup, U2 returned to
Europe for the remaining few weeks of the decade. Bono had been experiencing trouble with his voice, and while in Germany it gave out.
U2 had to cancel two shows in Amsterdam and it gave him time to
think if he would be able to sustain the hectic pace of touring into his
30s and beyond. Of course, others had been able to so, but Bono's style
was more physical than Bowie's or Jagger's.

U2 returned to Ireland for four New Year's shows at Dublin's Point
Depot. Bono considered these to be milestones, and they provided him
time to reflect back on the past decade and understand U2's trajectory.
He said, "If I'm honest this was the end of a journey that Bob Dylan had
sent us on. In 1985, sitting backstage at his concert in Slane Castle,
he said to me, 'You've got to go back. You've got to understand the
roots.'"[5]

Bono was right. Everything that had occurred for U2 since that
meeting was a response to Dylan's advice. Not only musically—fruits
of which could be seen in *Rattle and Hum*—but also politically in
U2's embrace of progressive politics in reaction to what was to become 12 years of Republican conservative government in the United
States. Bono's personal views were in the same tradition as his heroes
from the 1960s, Martin Luther King Jr. and John Lennon. Now, as he
looked back on the 1980s, he understood that U2 had misfired with
Rattle and Hum by not making a more conscious effort to confront
their own times, not just politically and musically, but also in terms of
the technology available and the media. Both of these key factors—
technology and the media—were shaping the era in ways like never
before. As Bono left the stage in Dublin in the first early hours of
1990, he was acutely aware that one stage was ending and another
would soon begin in the creative life of U2. What was to come had
yet to be determined.

Early in the year, Bono and Edge agreed to take on a new project
that would take them in a different direction from their present roles
in U2. The classic Anthony Burgess novel, *A Clockwork Orange,* was
being turned into a theatrical production by London's famed Royal
Shakespeare Company and the duo had been commissioned to write
the score. It proved to be a daunting task, especially since Stanley
Kubrick's 1971 film was believed to include the definitive soundtrack

composed by American electronic musician, Walter Carlos, aka Wendy Carlos. As a result, Bono and Edge took Carlos's template as their starting point and attempted to update it with techno and industrial music serving as their base. Bono had been turning away from classic rock and listening to the more aggressive contemporary sounds of Nine Inch Nails, Front 242, and German post-industrialist band, Einstürzende Neubauten. The final score left much to be desired and it failed to capture the tension at the heart of Burgess's novel, who dismissed the music as "neo-wallpaper."[6]

Nevertheless, it turned out to be a valuable learning experience and a vital introduction to musical styles that were the antithesis of what U2 had explored in *Rattle and Hum*. Rather than look to the United States, this music was European, modern, and relied on technology that was much more sophisticated. The themes of violence and decadence conveyed in Burgess's novel were also closer to what Bono's early musical heroes like Bowie and the Clash had expressed. *A Clockwork Orange* helped Bono get beyond *Rattle and Hum* and look to the future where he could use more theatrics and irony to get a point across. Those were some of the devices Burgess had used, which Bono recognized as giving the work more impact.

In March, Bono and Ali rented a van and drove across the United States with their newborn daughter. Bono did a lot of writing and finished two songs for the Neville Brothers. It was a good opportunity to explore writing in a different style, which he had successfully done before for Roy Orbison. He was considering many different approaches and even started noticing the word "baby" creeping into his lyrics for the first time in his life. Having a child and spending time with his family was an enriching experience, and as he was approaching 30 he was beginning to understand the meaning of responsibility.

After returning to Dublin he and Edge worked on a Cole Porter song, "Night and Day," for the AIDS benefit compilation, *Red Hot and Blue*. U2 often used cover songs as a chance to explore radical interpretations of the original and explore different approaches that they may not have done with their own originals. "Night and Day" was quite a radical departure from anything they had done since *The Unforgettable Fire*. The production was murky and suggestive and reflected the new influences Bono and Edge were listening to.

Throughout early 1990, the news was focused on the former Soviet Union and its satellites in Eastern Europe. The Berlin Wall had fallen only a few months before and events were moving fast. It looked as though the West had won the battle of ideologies and that Communism was being swept away. Musically, bands were taking their cues from the house and club scenes forming around "MADchester" with the Happy Mondays and Stone Roses leading the way. All these influences were coalescing into a distinctive aesthetic that was also heavily influenced by American rap and hip-hop bands like Public Enemy and De La Soul. Overnight, U2 was beginning to look like relics from a bygone era, but Bono, like a champion contender, was readying himself for a comeback. He wanted the band to relocate to Berlin, newly liberated and undergoing unification, to capture some of this spirit for U2's new material. The rest of the band wasn't convinced and while they liked the idea, practically it seemed impossible to pull off. Bono had recovered from the *Rattle and Hum* letdown and was ready once again to take the band to places it had never imagined. He pressed on and finally Paul agreed to drive across Europe to Berlin and check out the situation. After arriving, he reported back that the city was indeed exploding with excitement about the future, but it was also like an old suit, worn and in need of much repair. He had checked out the famous Hansa studio where Bowie and Eno had collaborated in the late 1970s on albums *Heroes, Low,* and *Lodger,* and it was available.

It was an exhilarating prospect and Bono couldn't believe U2's luck. If they went, the band could tap into the zeitgeist and record in one of the most exciting cities in the world. But family was a concern. Bono felt domesticity conflicted with his creative life. He had now been home for close to a year and he was itching for a change. After much deliberation and discussion about family and the worries of being separated, they packed up and flew to Berlin on October 3, 1990, exactly the same day the two Germanys officially reunited. They checked into a hotel in former East Berlin and began to set up at Hansa. The studio had originally been used as a Nazi ballroom, and since the late 1970s, when Eno had worked there, it had fallen into disrepair and neglect. As Bono recalled:

What we thought were just hairline cracks that could be easily fixed turned out to be more serious, the walls needed underpinning, we had to put down new foundations or the house would fall down. In fact it was falling down all around us. We were running up hotel bills and we had professional people, the U2 crew, staring at our averageness and scratching their heads and wondering if maybe they'd have been better off working for Bruce Springsteen. We came face to face with our limitations as a group on a lot of levels, playing and songwriting. When you're at sea the smartest thing to do is to find some dry land as quick as possible. So I think Larry and Adam were just anxious: "Stop messing around with all this electronica, let's get back to doing what we do. Because all this experimental stuff isn't working very well, is it? And, by the way, *Clockwork Orange* was (expletive)." There was a bit of that going on. "Did somebody say we were a rock band?" As you were walking down the corridor, you'd overhear that kind of remark.[7]

Bono and Edge were working feverishly on new material using drum machines and samples to sketch out their ideas. Larry wasn't too happy with the setup and was questioning whether or not the band would continue recording the album this way. If they did, he could see that his role in the production was going to be minimal at best. He sulked in the background until Bono reassured him. U2 would always be a band despite a few differences once in a while. A split was emerging within the group, nonetheless, with Bono and Edge on one side and Larry and Adam on the other. Bono had become intent on abandoning everything to do with *The Joshua Tree*, turning away from the past and embracing the future. Adam and Larry thought it was foolish to reject the band's strengths and argued for continuity. Disagreements were threatening to sink the band. As Bill Flanagan wrote, "It has never been this hard for U2 before. The band members begin to consider that they really have reached the end of the line together, that *Rattle and Hum* was the start of a downhill slide they'd best be off halting before it goes any further."[8]

Despite the differences in vision, they had agreed to work again with Eno and Lanois. One area in which there was little dispute was their conclusion about what had gone wrong with *Rattle and Hum*. The consensus was they had become complacent and lost focus. They knew themselves well enough to know that without a strong hand they could easily become distracted. They also needed someone who knew what they could do.

Lanois was the first to arrive before Eno, and he immediately went to work listening to the demos the band had come up with and picking out selections that he thought were promising. He soon revealed himself to be on the same page as Bono and Edge and was eager to put the axe to *The Joshua Tree*, but that didn't mean he shared their interest in drum machines and programming. He recognized U2's power was as a collective band and that their sound needed to remain rooted in the basics before considering effects.

With international fame, there came interesting opportunities and invitations. Tibet's Dalai Lama asked U2 if they would be interested in playing a concert called "Oneness," but Bono recoiled at the idea. From his dismissal came the idea for a lyric:

> The words just fell out of the sky, a gift. We had a request from the Dalai Lama to participate in a festival called Oneness. I love and respect the Dalai Lama but there was something a little bit "let's hold hands" hippie to me about this particular event. I am in awe of the Tibetan position on non-violence but this event didn't strike a chord. I sent him back a note saying, "One—but not the same."[9]

As the band rehearsed in the studio, all four together bouncing ideas off one another as they had always done, the structure of "One" emerged. They suddenly began to feel that things were beginning to move in the right direction. Bono knew the song was special and Lanois too was excited to see the old magic still at work. Over three years had passed since he had worked in the studio with the band and he knew a lot could change in that time. When Eno finally arrived, he listened to the demos they had assembled and gave pithy but extremely useful feedback. He liked what he was hearing except for one track— "One." He hated it. This was exactly what Bono had missed; someone who questioned the consensus and forced the band to examine their assumptions. As a result, the band went back to the drawing board and pushed and pulled the song apart until it reached the level it eventually attained as one of the band's greatest achievements.

In early 1991, U2 returned to Dublin to continue working on the new album. War had broken out in Iraq and it was being broadcast on cable news around the world 24 hours a day. People were gathering together in front of the TV as they would for a sports event to watch missiles flashing and flaring through the air until they hit their targets. It resembled some kind of video game and successfully detached the viewer from the ruins of war. Bono was sickened by the effect but also fascinated by what media and technology could accomplish. As he switched from one channel to the next from the comfort of his sofa in Dublin, he was gaining a new understanding of the power of the media. He would use the conflict and the representation of it for inspiration to write new songs.

While in Dublin, U2 continued working on the new material with engineer Mark Ellis, aka Flood, who had also worked on *The Joshua Tree* sessions. Ali was pregnant and on July 7, 1991, she gave birth to the couple's second daughter, Memphis Eve. Things were changing quickly and Bono was now a father of two young girls. His lyrics reflected all these changes and he plumbed the depths of his feelings to conjure up ideas for songs.

After U2 had scored with "One," the process ran smoother than Bono had anticipated. He began to adopt personas in his songs. The lyrics seemed to come more easily when imagining scenarios these characters might experience. "The Fly" was an obnoxious and belligerent figure, a self-aggrandizing boar masked in wrap-around shades. The songs were more enigmatic and elliptical than anything U2 had done before, and Bono was having fun impersonating the characters. He was looking forward to the next tour and began to assemble a costume for his stage persona: "The rock star I put together for myself was an identi-kit. I had Elvis Presley's leather jacket, Jim Morrison's leather pants, Lou Reed's shades, Jerry Lee Lewis's boots, Gene Vincent's limp. You want rock 'n' roll stuff? I'll give you some."[10]

Other songs like "So Cruel" and "Love Is Blindness" were intensely penetrating songs about the pain inherent in the most intimate of relationships. Rather than address global issues of social import, Bono was willing to take some of John Lennon's favorite adages, "Think globally, act locally" and "the personal is political." He was also being influenced by postmodern critiques of the media. In "Even Better than the Real Thing," he interrogated the nature of reality:

> So with these new eyes that we had, we thought "Even Better than the Real Thing" is actually where people live right now. People are no longer after experiences of truth. They want to know, "What is the point?" And the point is the moment. That's where we live right now, in this rave culture.[11]

As recording was coming to an end in the summer of 1991, Bono recognized that the material was just as good as *The Joshua Tree*. While kicking around ideas for album titles, Bono felt that the title shouldn't take itself too seriously. When *Achtung Baby* came up, he felt it was a perfect fit: "It's probably the heaviest record we've ever made. There is a lot of blood and guts on that record. It tells you a lot about packaging, because the press would have killed us if we'd called it anything else."[12]

That was U2's attitude as the album was being finished. The band felt as though the media were ready to dismiss anything they released, and they were trying hard to upset expectations and create something completely different. The pressure was on, but it was mostly self-inflicted. The band was driven to exceed what they had done before, if not in sales, then in quality.

Anticipation was growing, but Paul was careful not to leak anything to the press and released information through its fan magazine, *Propaganda*. "The Fly" was released as a single in October with its accompanying video and it established Bono's fly persona that he would take on for the upcoming Zoo TV tour. Bono described the song as "the sound of four men chopping down *The Joshua Tree*."[13] It eventually reached number one in the United Kingdom, bumping Bryan Adam's "Everything I Do" from the top spot, but failed to break into the Top 50 in the United States. North America was still behind the curve when it came to industrial and techno and the grunge scene was in full flight at the time. "Mysterious Ways" was the next single released five weeks later with a stunning video shot in Morocco and directed by Stéphane Sednaoui. He had just produced the highly successful video for "Give It Away" by the Red Hot Chili Peppers. As Bono said, "We want to make a record that pushes out the boundaries a bit, not just for ourselves but in terms of what people are used to hearing on the radio or on records. We want to start abusing the technology that's available."[14]

The album finally hit the racks in November and it was instantly greeted with rave reviews. *Rolling Stone* gave it 4.5 stars out of 5 and the general consensus was that U2 had proven it could evolve and survive into a new decade at the vanguard of popular music. The music was richly textured, murky, sexy, and suggestive in ways that had only been hinted at before in tracks such as "With or Without You" or "All I Want Is You." This time around, Bono's voice conveyed more menace and sensuality and had overtaken his choirboy tenor. From the kaleido-scopic collage of the Anton Corbijn cover to Edge's burnished effects, everything seemed new. U2 had succeeded in reinventing themselves on record; now it was time to prove it onstage. *Achtung Baby* debuted in the United States at number one and set the band up to mount a world tour in the New Year.

NOTES

1. "Bono's Grammy's Speech in 1988 for Album of the Year," http://www.angelfire.com/band2/u2megbael/interviews/bonogrammy88.html.

2. Tony Clayton-Lea, *U2 Popaganda: Essential U2 Quotations* (Dublin: Hodder Headline Ireland, 2007), 153.

3. Carter Alan, *Outside Is America: U2 in the US* (Boston: Faber and Faber, 1992), 192.

4. Bill Flanagan, *U2 at the End of the World* (London: Bantam Press, 1995), 5.

5. *U2 by U2* (New York: HarperCollins, 2006), 213.

6. "Poor Reviews for Musical of 'A Clockwork Orange,'" *New York Times*, February 14, 1990, http://www.nytimes.com/1990/02/14/theater/poor-reviews-for-musical-of-a-clockwork-orange.html.

7. "'U2ByU2': A Portrait by the Artists," *USA Today*, September 22, 2006, http://www.usatoday.com/life/music/news/2006-09-21-U2-book_x.htm.

8. Flanagan, *U2 at the End of the World*, 7–8.

9. "'U2ByU2': A Portrait by the Artists."

10. Michka Assayas, *Bono on Bono* (London: Hodder & Stoughton, 2005), 39.

11. Niall Stokes, *U2: Into the Heart* (London: Carlton Books, 2005), 189.

12. Rolling Stone, *U2: The Ultimate Compendium of Interviews, Articles, Facts and Opinions* (New York: Hyperion, 1994), 184

13. "The Fly," u2.com, http://www.u2.com/discography/index/album/albumId/4037/tagName/Singles.

14. Clayton-Lea, *U2 Popaganda*, 63.

Chapter 6

BETTER BY DESIGN: BACK ON TRACK (1992–1995)

As fellow Irishman Oscar Wilde was fond of saying, "The mask reveals the man." Bono relished the opportunity to perform as different characters onstage. He began to wear wraparound shades, covering his eyes, and a leather suit like the one Jim Morrison and Gene Vincent before him had worn. Bono looked anything but the same man who had earnestly sung about searching for what he was looking for; he was now in the mood to fully enjoy the ride:

> There were reports of egomania, and I just decided to become everything they said I was. Might as well . . . I felt like I didn't recognize the person I was supposed to be, as far as what you saw in the media. There's some kind of rape that happens when you are in the spotlight, and you go along with it . . . I used to think that if you just had enough time you could get it right. You could just say, "Well, this isn't true, no, no, that isn't so." But this machine is so hungry that you can't. You can just feed it. So what we're doing is like misinformation.[1]

After the album was released, Bono put his energy into planning for the Zoo TV tour along with set designer Willie Williams. U2 purchased a huge vidi-wall and began collecting images and epigrams to show on the screen. It would be like theater, a genuine performance, or an art installation, and Bono would have the ability to control the images with a handheld remote control. Looking back on the tour in 2006, journalist Adrian Deevoy wrote,

> Television, you see, was a problem and it needed looking at. The remote control of reason had slipped down behind the sofa of sanity and the viewing public was paying the price. We were the walking wounded in the schedule wars, the victims of a messy TV OD. So what were we to do about the sinister box in the corner? Rage against it like Peter Finch in Network, kick it over like Travis Bickle or shoot it out like Elvis? Cue U2.[2]

Zoo TV opened at the end of February in Lakeland, Florida, and it was a frontal assault, a true media blitz in Bono's hands that he would play and interact with by changing channels. He also used a phone from the stage. He once called the White House and tried to get through to President Bush and another time he ordered 1,000 pizzas. One hundred were actually delivered. After a few weeks, the tour began to take on different characteristics, with the band hiring a belly dancer and Bono wearing different costumes that reflected his different personas. He would change into gold and silver lamé suits for his dual characters, Mr. MacPhisto and Mirror Ball Man. He was exploring all facets of his personality: "I want heaven and hell. We've always been given this choice, to choose between the flesh and the spirit. I don't know anyone who isn't both."[3]

Epigrams like "Everything You Know Is Wrong" or "Watch More TV" would flash across the different screens at lightning speed creating a strobing effect. The cumulative overload was overwhelming, but also thrilling. The tour crossed the Atlantic to begin its European leg in Paris in May. When U2 arrived in London, Bono met the author Salman Rushdie and the two hit it off. Bono harbored a desire to write books and Rushdie had been a huge music fan and secretly desired being a rock star. Rushdie had been living undercover since 1988 when his novel *The Satanic Verses* inspired a fatwa against his life from Iran's Ayatollah Khomeini. Bono would later invite Rushdie to Ireland to stay at his home.

While U2 was in England, they decided to use their celebrity to support Greenpeace and joined the green group aboard the ship *Solo*. They traveled to Sellafield to protest against the building of a nuclear power plant and to highlight the issue of radioactive contamination. Social issues were still a part of U2's agenda and they were branching out to support more causes, but the tour was financially taxing:

> We were risking bankruptcy. You see, Zoo TV cost so much . . . it cost a quarter of a million dollars a day to take that thing around. So, if ten percent less people had come to see us, we'd have gone bankrupt, and with those kinds of bills, you don't go bankrupt a little, you go bankrupt a lot. . . . I remember speaking to Ali about the consequences of failure. She was fearless: "What's the worst, to sell the house, and get a smaller one . . . what's wrong with that? . . ." That's the only time I actually thought about failure. I never thought about it up to that.[4]

When U2 returned to the United States in the summer of 1992 for the second leg of Zoo TV, they found themselves in the middle of a U.S. election that was pitting incumbent Republican president George H. W. Bush against the Democratic newcomer Bill Clinton. It was no secret where Bono's sympathies lay. Every night he took to the stage accompanied by a clip parodying Bush singing "We Will Rock You."

When the tour landed in Chicago, U2 coincidentally booked into the same hotel as Clinton and a visit was arranged between Bono and Clinton:

> A great leader has to have a great ear for melody. By this, I mean clarity of ideas. What I think they might all have in common, the ones I've met—if they're any good—is an ability to see through the din and clangour of ideas and conversations and points of view, and hear the melody line, and realise: this is the thing we've got to do; this is more important than the others. They're like talent scouts in (ok) the music business, A&R men for ideas. Bill Clinton was incredible at spotting an idea.[5]

Bono was learning how to network with people in high places such as politicians and business executives, whether in the music or political

sectors. He had always been a smooth talker and radiated genuine interest in others, which opened doors and generated opportunities. Now
that he was more mature, he was exploring how to connect with real
power-players and think about how he could bring these people together to make an impact on the causes he and U2 cared about. Bono
was never satisfied with just being an entertainer or a rock singer—
he wanted to serve something larger and exploit his fame to influence
world events in a positive way.

The Zoo TV tour was making a huge celebrity out of Bono, more
than during previous tours. He was invited to pose for the cover of
British Vogue with model Christy Turlington and became the first man
to do so in 20 years. In November, Bill Clinton won the election and
became the first Democrat to take the White House in 12 years. A few
months later, U2 was invited to the inauguration, but Bono couldn't
make it, opting to stay in Dublin with family instead.

During the break between tours, Bono was eager to record some of
the new songs that the band had left over from the *Achtung Baby* sessions, but they only had 12 weeks. Bono pushed for making an entire
album and convinced the rest of the band it could be done. He felt
they were playing at their best and the momentum and sound they had
established was worth capturing on a new album. While in the middle
of recording, Johnny Cash's tour came to Dublin and Bono, Edge, and
Larry joined him onstage at the Olympia. The next day Cash was invited to the studio to record the vocal track of a new song that would
become "The Wanderer."

A new album gave the band a chance to utilize the technical profi-
ciency they had learned while working on *Achtung Baby* and it was why
Bono believed they could quickly record another quality album. At the
end of February, *Achtung Baby* won a Grammy for Best Vocal Performance but lost Album of the Year to Eric Clapton's *Unplugged*. Eno and
Flood were helping with the new material, but by May when the European tour began, they weren't finished and had to make contingency
plans. They decided they would fly home to Dublin every night to put
the finishing touches on the songs. It was a grueling schedule, but the
band rose to the challenge and finished the album in June. Meanwhile,
their tour had also evolved adding new dimensions and references.
Each concert would open with a clip from Leni Reifenstahl's *Triumph*

of the Will, with the thundering sounds of marching drummers filling the air. Images of swastikas were also inserted during "Bullet the Blue Sky." For Bono's 33rd birthday his old friend Gavin Friday gave him an eight-foot cross, painted blue, with "Hail Bono, King of the Zoos" inscribed on it.

The tour was getting great reviews and Bono could feel that the band had reached a higher level and were at the peak of their powers. He was enjoying the performances like never before. He felt like a genuine artist expressing the different shades of his character with provocative gestures and images taken from decades of pop culture.

In July, just before the new album was to be released, U2 renewed their contract with Island Records making them the highest-paid band in rock history. The deal was for six albums worth $60 million, plus a $10 million advance for each album, and a 25 percent royalty rate for every album sold. Bono had reason to rejoice.

Zooropa, U2's eighth studio album, was released on July 5, 1993. A pun on "Europe," the album title and cover art were references to the European Union, which was scheduled to be formally established in November of that year. Bono's opening lyrics were borrowed from German carmaker Audi: "Vorsprung durch Technik," which translated as "advancement through technology," revealing U2's new manifesto.

In an interview with *Hot Press* prior to the album's release, Bono said, "Religion is the enemy of God . . . it denies the spontaneity of the spirit."[6] Over the years, he had come to view his faith differently than in the early days. He still regarded himself as a Christian but had become increasingly suspicious of organized religions: "I have to accept that one of the things that I picked up from my father and my mother was the sense that religion often gets in the way of God."[7]

While touring and living in the United States, Bono saw firsthand how religion had been manipulated for personal profit through the examples of corrupt televangelists like Jim Baker and Jimmy Swaggart. He had also seen how belonging exclusively to any one organization limited his ability to express his ideas freely. Like other believers, Bono had to forge his own personal faith and viewed religion as stifling individuality. He was also reading a lot of American literature and was inspired by the poetry of Charles Bukowski. "Dirty Day" was written for him after the two had met backstage in Los Angeles, having been introduced by mutual friend Sean Penn. "The Wanderer" had been written with the book of Ecclesiastes in mind and was also known as "The Preacher." When Bono discovered that Johnny Cash was available, he reworked the lyrics to reflect the Old Testament demeanor of the "Man in Black." Another prominent influence on the new album was German director Wim Wenders. He had asked Bono to write something for his upcoming film, *Faraway, So Close*. Bono and Edge came up with "Stay (Faraway, So Close)," which became the album's third single. To highlight the band's new sound, "Numb" was chosen as the album's first single, followed by "Lemon." These two songs highlighted Edge as the main vocalist with Bono adding falsetto and Brian Eno lending support on "Lemon." They were radical departures, more so than anything on *Achtung Baby* and they helped form the band's image as risk takers who were unafraid of taking chances. Critics agreed and Anthony DeCurtis from *Rolling Stone* called it "daring" awarding it 4 out of 5 stars.

As the European tour continued, U2 was receiving information about the conflict raging in the Balkans, and they decided they had to do something. Bono met with filmmaker and activist Bill Carter, who had been doing work in Sarajevo, and he suggested U2 perform in the city to bring attention to the war that was engulfing the region. Bono was moved to tears by what Carter was telling him and he agreed to visit. When Paul heard the news, he reminded Bono of the terrible risks at hand. He suggested the band arrange a video link from the capital and broadcast it at their concerts as an alternative to playing live in the war-torn city and Bono agreed. These video feeds featured Carter and others, mainly victims or those who had suffered from the violence. They become somber moments in the shows and often sucked the energy out of the songs that followed. When one particular interview at the Glasgow show almost ruined the entire concert, the band decided to can the feeds. U2 was in danger of taking themselves too seriously once again and turning off fans who didn't come to a concert to be confronted with the horrors of war. Bono slipped back into his Mac-Phisto persona, and when Salman Rushdie was invited onstage Bono relished the chance to joke about *The Satanic Verses* being his own work. He addressed the audience: "Rock 'n' roll—it's the new religion, rock & roll. I have a great interest in religion. Some of my best friends are religious leaders. The ayatollah, the pope, even the Archbishop of Canterbury—I think he's fabulous. They're doing my work for me. . . . Nobody's going to church anymore."[8]

U2 ended the tour in Dublin at the end of August and Bono went to work on recording a duet of "I Got You under My Skin" with Frank Sinatra. Like Elvis, Sinatra was a legend and a larger-than-life figure, but he had survived the ravages of fame to become celebrated by a new generation. Sinatra was putting together a new album of duets with a number of contemporary singers and Bono was included. He recorded his part separately in Dublin, but a few months later in November the two united to shoot the video. Bono flew into Palm Springs and Sinatra joked that he thought he was doing the duet with Sonny Bono. To show his gratitude, Sinatra sent Bono a Cartier platinum and sapphire Pasha watch.[9] Bono was thrilled and knew his mother would have been genuinely impressed that he had met and sang with "Ol' Blue Eyes" himself. Bono saw himself as the modern-day version of crooners like Sinatra and opportunities like this were not only a chance to pay tribute but also to learn something about the craft of singing from one of the 20th century's masters.

The next leg of the tour opened in Australia in November for the "Zoomerang" and "Noo Zealand" tours. The plan was to capture the experience on film in Sydney. Arrangements were made for director David Mallet to film two shows, back to back, and choose the best bits from each. The night before the first show Adam got drunk and disappeared. Larry was finally able to reach him a few hours before showtime but Adam was in no condition to perform. Luckily, Adam's bass technician, Stuart Morgan, played bass and knew the parts well enough that he could substitute. The band was shocked. No one had ever missed the call of duty before and a meeting was held as soon as possible. Adam felt terrible and also feared for his future with U2. He apologized, admitted he had hit rock bottom, and vowed to seek help to deal with his alcohol problem. The next evening he performed like a professional as though nothing had happened. The film version was taken entirely from this second concert.

The next stop was Japan for the final dates of Zoo TV. U2 was being supported by an old hero, the Clash's Mick Jones, who was now with his own band, BAD. As Bono walked the streets of Tokyo amid its flashing neon and giant video screens, he felt as though he was in the heart of the beast, the capital and technological nerve center of the Zoo Nation. It was an apt conclusion to three frenetic and wildly successful years.

When Bono returned home, he sought refuge and comfort with family and friends. A normal tour is usually a disorientating experience, but Zoo TV had ground on for three years and included two new albums, videos, and a film. It took Bono a long time to decompress and get used to living a regular life with Ali and his two daughters. Ali suggested he stay in a hotel for his first week back in Dublin: "I don't want to, but Ali says it's better. A couple of days after I get back to Dublin we've got to be on a TV special. It will just confuse the kids if I come home and start working again right away, and she says they'll be hurt if they talk to me and I don't hear them."[10]

In January, he gave the induction speech at the Rock and Roll Hall of Fame for one of his spiritual and musical heroes, Bob Marley. Growing up, Bono wasn't too familiar with reggae music beyond Eric Clapton's "I Shot the Sheriff," and it wasn't until his relationship with Chris Blackwell and Island Records began in 1980 that he started to pay attention. He had spent time in Jamaica over the years and came to appreciate reggae, particularly identifying with Rastafarianism's independent interpretation of Christianity that posited Africa as a spiritual homeland. Marley was like a shaman with a direct conduit to God and Bono viewed his songs as psalms, spiritual meditations on the condition of humanity in relation to the almighty creator. He also identified with being a fellow "Island man":

> I know claiming Bob Marley is Irish might be a little difficult here tonight, but bear with me. Jamaica and Ireland have a lot in common: Naomi Campbell, Chris Blackwell, Guinness, a fondness for little greenleaves—the weed. Religion. The philosophy of procrastination—don't put off til tomorrow what you can put off til the day after. Unless, of course, it's freedom. We are both islands; we were both colonies. We share a common yoke: the struggle for identity, the struggle for independence, the vulnerable and uncertain future that's left behind when the jackboot of empire has finally retreated.

Well, Bob Marley didn't choose or walk down the middle. He raced to the edges, embracing all extremes, creating a oneness. His oneness. One love. He wanted everything at the same time. Prophet. Soul rebel. Rastaman. Herbsman. Wildman. A natural, mystic man. Lady's man. Island man. Family man. Rita's man. Soccer man. Showman. Shaman. Human. Jamaican![11]

Bono also showed up at the Grammys in New York City to give a tribute speech to Frank Sinatra, "the big bang of pop." Since collaborating on a duet the previous year, they had got to know each well enough to exchange gifts and call each other friend. For Bono, Sinatra represented America in its idealized form, the country that had joined Europe to defeat the Nazis and had come up with the Marshall Plan to reconstruct the continent after the war. Sinatra was the first pop star to become popular in the aftermath of World War II, and he embodied the swagger of Elvis and the suavity of crooners like Tony Bennett. For Bono, Sinatra was America in the 20th century, a living myth:

Rock and Roll people love Frank Sinatra because Frank has got what we want: swagger and attitude; he's big on attitude Serious attitude, bad attitude Frank's the Chairman of the bad Rock and Roll plays at being tough but this guy, well, he's the boss

The boss of bosses
The man
The big bang of pop
I'm not gonna mess with him, are you?[12]

Bono was thinking of new ways for U2 to write and record in comfort. He proposed the idea of purchasing a few houses in the south of France near Nice for the band to assemble and rehearse without making difficult alterations to their schedules. Each family could gather together living in a communal lifestyle while relaxing and still fulfilling U2's commitments. In the end, Edge was the only one who shared the same vision, and they bought property with two houses in the village of Eze. They gathered in the summer of 1994 and spent the summer playing music and hosting friends such as INXS's lead singer, Michael

Hutchence. Brit-pop bands like Oasis and Blur were in full bloom and Bono was indulging in the new bands while plotting U2's next move. It would have to be a different project than *Zooropa* but still be accessible enough to compete with the bands of the day.

After the summer, Eno and U2 decided to work together on the soundtrack to Peter Greenaway's film *The Pillow Book*, but it fell through. Eno instead convinced the band to collaborate on a different project. They would put together an album where each song was to be a soundtrack for a fictional film. U2 spent two weeks with Eno in a London studio and the project eventually became known as *Original Soundtracks 1* and the pseudo-name for the collaboration became Passengers. The results were mixed and feelings in the band differed. Larry didn't like it, but Bono has called one of the songs, "Miss Sarajevo," his favorite U2 song.[13]

Bono chose to do a cover of Leonard Cohen's "Hallelujah" for a compilation to be released in the fall of 1995. He had come to Cohen in the late 1980s when he was enjoying renewed popularity for his album *I'm Your Man*. Bono fell under Cohen's spell and was in awe of his poetic powers and his ability to address the sacred and profane in a pop song. "Hallelujah" is one of Cohen's most famous songs and has inspired numerous covers, but none are quite as unique as Bono's. He chose to subvert the melody and put the emphasis on the spoken lyrics on top of a muted techno beat.

Throughout 1995, Bono and U2 worked on "Hold Me, Thrill Me, Kiss Me" for the *Batman Returns* soundtrack. Bono then traveled to Modena, Italy, for Luciano Pavarotti's charity concert. He performed with the legendary tenor on "Miss Sarajevo" along with Edge and Eno and then on an orchestral version of "One." Bono knew that his father would enjoy meeting Pavarotti, so he invited him along. After the performance, Bob was introduced to everyone, including Princess Diana, and he was visibly impressed. Seeing his father react this way was a rare thing for Bono to witness.

In the fall, Bono wrote a song for Ronny Drew from the Dubliners called "Drinkin' in the Day." The band was an institution around Ireland and was responsible for keeping alive the folk tradition. U2 had been fans of the group for years and had appeared in a Dubliners' special program back in 1987.

NOTES

1. David Schaffer, *Bono* (New York: Lucent Books, 2004), 70.

2. David Mallet, Director, *Zoo TV: Live From Sydney*, 1994.

3. Rolling Stone, *U2: The Ultimate Compendium of Interviews, Articles, Facts and Opinions* (New York: Hyperion, 1994), 188.

4. Michka Assayas, *Bono on Bono* (London: Hodder & Stoughton, 2005), 37–38.

5. Tony Clayton-Lea, *U2 Popaganda: Essential U2 Quotations* (Dublin: Hodder Headline Ireland, 2007), 52.

6. "Even Better Than the Surreal Thing," *Hot Press*, June 2, 1993, http://www.hotpress.com/archive/2613083.html.

7. Clayton-Lea, *U2 Popaganda*, 26.

8. Rolling Stone, *U2*, 210.

9. *U2 by U2* (New York: HarperCollins, 2006), 255.

10. Bill Flanagan, *U2 at the End of the World* (London: Bantam Press, 1995), 142.

11. "Bono Inducts Bob Marley into the Rock and Roll Hall of Fame," U2 Station, January 19, 1994, http://www.u2station.com/news/archives/1994/01/bono_inducts_bo.php.

12. "Bono Introduces Frank Sinatra at the Grammy Awards," Spirit of Sinatra Blog, March 1, 1994, http://www.spiritofsinatra.com/pages/about.html.

13. "Just the 2 of U," *Irish Times*, February 27, 2009, http://www.irishtimes.com/newspaper/theticket/2009/0227/1224241848766.html.

Chapter 7

STARING AT THE SUN: CATCHING UP (1996–2000)

Now came time to focus on a new album. U2 and Eno agreed to take a break from one another and Flood, Howie B., and Steve Osbourne were asked to helm the mixing board. The band agreed that they wanted to create something new and relevant combining pop and club music. Bono had been listening to Massive Attack and the Prodigy and was getting bored with Brit-pop's recycled melodies. They decided the name of the album would be *Pop* and Bono felt the theme was about discovering beauty in unexpected places: "One of my definitions of art is the discovery of beauty in unexpected places. This was really the theme of *Pop*: big subjects for the basement."[1]

Paul went ahead and booked the next tour thinking everything was running on schedule, but he forgot that U2 worked at its own pace. They were spending more time than they thought on creating the right sonics and rhythms that would cross over from dance floors to radio. Bono felt they had succeeded on the opening song, "Discothèque," a trashy dance song that was unlike anything U2 had done before. The band felt like they needed a break and in May they flew to Miami. They blew off steam while exploring the nightlife and culture of Florida's largest city. Bono was doing a lot of writing and recording events, which eventually led to the creation of the song "Miami." The band returned to Dublin in early May when their old friend, the journalist Bill Graham, passed away. He had been one of the first journalists to recognize U2's potential when they were just starting out and he gave them their first write-up in *Hot Press*.

Recording continued and deadlines were looming. Bono had written a song about his mother called "Mofo," going so far as to ask, "Mother, am I still your son?" She was still a major factor in Bono's life. He often wrote about her and reflected on her influence and on his feelings regarding her loss: "It was if my whole life was in that song. Electronic blues death rattle. It takes the cliché insult 'motherf***ker' and turns it into something raw and confessional. It went though some bizarre titles—Mothership, Oedipussy . . ."[2]

Some of the other songs in the album had a real pop sound, which Bono was hoping for:

> I thought "pop" was a term of abuse, it seemed sort of insulting and lightweight. I didn't realise how cool it was. Because some of the best music does have a lightweight quality, it has a kind of oxygen in it, which is not to say it's emotionally shallow. We've had to get the brightly coloured wrapping paper right, because what's underneath is not so sweet.[3]

"Staring at the Sun" and "If God Will Send His Angels" were perfect slices of pop tailor-made for mainstream play. The closing song, "Wake Up Dead Man," was a dark song about redemption Bono collaborated on with Edge, who wrote the chorus and first verse.

The first single was "Discothèque" and for the video they hired Stéphane Sednaoui once again. It was a disco theme and the band dressed up as Village People extras, grinding for the camera inside a mirror ball. Released in January 1997, a month before the album was due, it revealed a band in transition once again and raised some eyebrows as to what U2 was up to. When the album was finally released in February 1997, it got mixed reviews but reached number 1 in 27 countries. Much criticism had to do with the mixed genres and inconsistent production from song to song. The band's look was also challenging and exuded a kitschy suavity with polyester suits and gold chains. Looking back, Bono realized the album had its flaws: "We wanted to make a party record but we came in at the end of the party. The dancing was over and there were a load of broken bottles and young people sleeping under tables and the odd row in the garden between lovers who've imbibed too much."[4]

The band held a press conference at a New York City K-Mart department store to announce that the PopMart tour was scheduled to open in Las Vegas at the end of April. The tour was a huge investment and cost over $200,000 a day to run. Set designer Willie Williams worked with the band to incorporate images from consumer culture like the golden arches of McDonald's and branding images reminiscent of famous multinational companies. Bono wanted to go big and outdo Zoo TV, which would prove to be huge task. As a result, a 40-foot lemon and a 100-foot cocktail stick were designed as props. Despite all the publicity and the release of the album, U2 was having a hard time generating publicity and ticket sales for opening night. They tried producing a documentary on ABC television narrated by Dennis Hopper but it bombed as did their next single, "Staring at the Sun," which only reached to number 26 on Billboard.

When the tour finally opened on April 25, it suffered from technical glitches and revealed an ostentatious and garrulously attired U2. Bono wore bubble pants and a boxer's cape and pranced around the stage as though he was in a match against a huge, imaginary adversary. The awkward scenes persisted and within a few weeks some critics were calling the tour Flopmart. Bono felt confident that the show would improve as the band eased into a rhythm and became familiar with the dynamics and he was right. The tour got better over time and U2 started to include such covers into their sets as Neil Diamond's "Sweet Caroline" and the Monkees' "Daydream Believer."

During the American leg, U2 played with alternative bands like Sonic Youth and Rage against the Machine and when they hit the West Coast, chart rivals Oasis supported their shows. During the tour Bono got a chance to meet one of his literary heroes, William S. Burroughs. When they shot their video for "Last Night on Earth" Burroughs agreed to do a cameo.

In July, the tour crossed the Atlantic and the European leg opened in the Netherlands. They started drawing larger crowds and were generally better received. But the tour was still subject to problems, and in Oslo as the band was getting ready to take the stage their giant lemon refused to open, trapping them inside. They eventually had to exit from the back. Paul explained how he felt:

> Utter panic. But also a feeling of immense relief that it was not me inside. I was standing there as it opened. It did open about a foot and I could see the 8 feet of my clients but not the rest of them. As I watched, they tried to close it first and open it again and it was well and truly jammed. It then made a retreat to its starting position and they had to climb out the back and out to the B stage. I really felt for them. It was, of course, the ultimate Spinal Tap moment.[5]

In August, the day after Princess Diana was killed in a car crash, U2 played in Dublin and they were swept up by the general media storm looking back on her life and influence. Bono had met her a few years before, but he took note of how she was able to use her celebrity status to draw attention to causes she supported such as the eradication of land mines and AIDS. Her example was something he would begin to model his own charity work on.

The war in the Balkans had stabilized enough by the summer of 1997 for U2 to commit to a concert in Sarajevo. When U2 arrived they were greeted like heroes and Muslims, Croats, and Serbs flocked to the battered Kosovo Stadium to hear the band perform. It was one of the most memorable nights for U2 and they let their exuberance shine through by adding Jimmy Cliff's "Many Rivers to Cross" and the Talking Heads' "Life during Wartime" to their set list. Bono also delivered what many regard as the definitive version of "One." As his voice was breaking up, Bono included the spoken line, "To be united is a great thing; but to respect differences maybe even a greater thing," which has since become one of his signature quotes.[6] Brian Eno also made the concert and joined the band to sing "Miss Sarajevo." They closed with "One" and "Unchained Melody," as the audience reluctantly filed out of the stadium.

Bono flashes a victory sign as he arrives at Sarajevo's airport, September 23, 1997. About 45,000 people were expected to pack the rebuilt Kosovo Olympic Stadium for the evening's concert, which fulfilled a pledge made by Bono when he spent the first postwar New Year's Eve with Sarajevans in December 1995, weeks after the war ended. (AP Photo/Sava Radovanovic)

U2 returned to North America in October and were confronted with hardships once again. Howie B. was kicked off the tour when he was caught at the U.S. border with a small amount of marijuana. When the band reached Tampa Bay they played to only 20,000 fans in a stadium that could accommodate over three times that many. It felt like their connection to the United States was withering away. The tour moved south to Mexico City where they had planned to record the show for a video that became *PopMart: Live from Mexico City*. An unfortunate event occurred. President Ernesto Zedillo's two sons arrived at the concert unannounced without tickets and forced their way in, causing injury to members of U2's security. The next day the president called for a meeting. Thinking an apology would be forthcoming, U2 attended but instead he accused the band of inflicting harm on his sons. The band was shocked and it would take two years before the incident was settled in U2's favor when Jerry Mele, U2's head of security, won a substantial settlement in a 1999 court case.

After a Christmas break, PopMart continued to South America, where U2 played their first-ever concerts in Argentina, Chile, and

Brazil. It was an opportunity for U2 to show their support to the Mothers de Plaza de Mayo, the group who kept alive the memories of those who had perished in Argentina's "Dirty War." The shows ended with "Mothers of the Disappeared" as the women recited the names of their loved ones. In Chile, the response was different as the country was divided over the legacy of Pinochet, the tyrannical general who ruled from 1973 to 1990. Some members of the audience booed Bono's emotional plea for Pinochet to "give the dead back to the living."[7]

After finishing in South America, the tour traveled to Australia where Bono summed up PopMart's intent: "The job of rock 'n' roll, if it has any kind of job at all, is to blow people's heads. It's a hard call to turn a shopping mall or a supermarket into a cathedral but that's actually what we're trying to do. We're trying to find the spirit in the machine, if you like."[8]

During each concert, Bono would dedicate "One" to old friend Michael Hutchence from INXS who had recently committed suicide. U2 also covered "Never Tear Us Apart" in his memory, with Bono adding, "This is his country. This is his house and we can't help thinking about him when we're here."[9] The tour then traveled to Japan where it finally wrapped up. The tour made the *Guinness Book of World Records* for playing to the largest audience at the time—3.9 million—while *Pop* had sold a total of 7 million copies.

When Bono settled back in Dublin, he started to get involved in the Northern Ireland peace process that had become a priority for the British and Irish governments. On Good Friday, April 10, 1998, a peace deal was reached between the parties and government in Northern Ireland that would change the Irish constitution to make it mutually acceptable for all interested. A referendum on whether or not to accept this agreement was scheduled for May 22. U2's position had always been in favor of the talks, and when the agreement was announced the band came out publicly on the side of the Yes campaign. The band had always considered themselves a microcosm of their own country with Edge and Adam being British and Bono and Larry being Irish.

They were asked to perform a few songs in support of the YES campaign at Belfast's Waterfront Hall a week before the referendum. They agreed but one condition Bono insisted on was that Ulster Unionist leader David Trimble and Social Democratic and Labour Party leader

John Hume join him onstage. Bono tried to recreate the iconic image of Bob Marley at the One Love Peace Concert in 1978 when Marley had asked rival politicians to join him onstage as a sign of good will. Bono has since called his involvement "the greatest honor" of his life.[10] A few days later the referendum passed in both the north and south, much to Bono's pleasure.

Bono had suffered throat problems from the early days of touring and he began to worry that it was something more serious. Then when his father was diagnosed with cancer it came as a very serious blow. Bob was getting older but he was a link to his mother and the life he knew when she was alive. He began to worry about his own health and without telling Ali, he got himself checked out for cancer. The results turned out to be negative and he could relax, but Bob started to undergo treatment and he continued to worry for his father. Ali was pregnant again with their third child and Bono was preoccupied with issues of life and death.

In the middle of August, a bomb went off in the Northern Irish town of Omagh, killing 29 and injuring 220 people. The so-called Real IRA claimed responsibility and it made international headlines as the worst incident of its kind since the beginning of the troubles 30 years before. Bono was heartbroken, especially since the victory of the Good Friday Agreement had only recently been achieved. He was moved to write about it and the song became "Peace on Earth," which would appear on U2's next album.

Later that year both David Trimble and John Hume won the Nobel Peace Prize and Bono hosted a dinner for them at his home. U2's relationship with Amnesty International was still strong and to kick off Amnesty's Irish campaign Bono addressed a crowd in downtown Dublin:

> One of the biggest problems in the world is the cynical idea that the world can't be changed and that politics and economics are too complicated to deal with. But with Amnesty it's simple; you can write a postcard and make a difference to the life of someone who is in jail or suffering human rights abuses.[11]

In September, U2 released an updated version of "The Sweetest Thing," a song they had originally included as a B-side to "Where the

Streets Have No Name" during *The Joshua Tree* sessions. The video was shot in the streets of Dublin with Kevin Godley directing. It follows a humorous narrative of Bono forgetting Ali's birthday and trying to make it up to her with various outrageous gifts. Although she was pregnant at the time, it wasn't noticeable in the video. It turned out to be one of their most popular songs and was a return to straight-ahead pop. It was included on their first greatest hits package, *The Best of U2: 1980–1990*, released in the fall of 1998.

As the year drew to a close, thoughts turned toward the recording of the next U2 album. Bono thought it was time to return to familiar territory, and he was keen to work with Eno and Lanois once again. Eno advised them to get into the studio as soon as possible, and they went into their own Hanover Quay studio and started throwing around ideas. Bono and the rest of the band agreed that a back-to-basics approach was necessary and they recorded like they did in the early days with only the four of them in the room. "Kite" was developed during these sessions. It was at this time that Bono discovered the cause for his throat problems; he had been suffering from allergies and his treatment involved medication that caused red eyes as a side effect. In response, he began to wear sunglasses on a regular basis.

In February1999, Bono and his old friend German director Wim Wenders began shooting the film *The Million Dollar Hotel*. Bono had got the idea back in 1987 when he saw an old hotel in Los Angeles with the same name and began developing a script based on who might be living inside such a provocatively named building. He was now determined to see the project through and got in touch with a screenwriter and secured Mel Gibson and Milla Jovovich to star. It took only 34 days to shoot and the film has the feel of an indie flick shot on the fly. But it moves quite slowly and was widely panned on its release. Even Gibson called it "as boring as a dog's arse."[12] The soundtrack was a bit more successful after Bono convinced Lanois and the rest of the band to collaborate on it. One of the best songs, "The Ground Beneath Her Feet," was cowritten with Salman Rushdie, who wrote the lyrics.

Bono's 40th birthday loomed about a year away and he was feeling restless. Since PopMart wound down, he had been looking for something beyond U2 to attach himself to in the way that he had with Amnesty and Band Aid in the 1980s. In February 1999, he wrote an editorial for the *Guardian* to launch the Jubilee 2000 campaign. It was an idea that was started earlier in the 1990s based on the biblical idea of Jubilee in Leviticus wherein debts are forgiven. It also coincided with the 2,000-year celebration of the Catholic Church known as the "Great Jubilee." The aim was to wipe out $90 billion of debt owed by the world's poorest nations, reducing the total to about $37 billion. Bono threw himself into the project and did everything he could along with other celebrities like old friend Bob Geldof and Radiohead's Thom Yorke. Bono said repeatedly that the effort wasn't about charity but about justice. As the movement grew, Bono began meeting with world leaders such as Tony Blair and Bill Clinton as well as famed philanthropist Eunice Shriver, John F. Kennedy's older sister. He was making an impact and a difference but U2 was being left behind and neglected. The band was ready with new songs but Bono was often out of town.

Bono not only was in demand for social justice issues but also was the first to be considered for tributes when his musician friends needed him. In the spring, it was Bruce Springsteen's turn to be inducted into the Rock and Roll Hall of Fame and Bono was happy to deliver the speech:

America was staggering when Springsteen appeared. The president had just resigned in disgrace, the U.S. had lost its first war, there was going to be no more oil in the ground, the days of cruising and big cars were supposed to be over. But Springsteen's vision was bigger than Honda. It was bigger than a Subaru. Bruce made you believe that dreams were still out there, but after loss and defeat. They had to be braver, not just bigger. He was singing, "Now you're scared, and you're thinking that maybe we ain't that young anymore," because it took guts to be romantic now. Knowing you could lose didn't mean you still didn't take the ride. In fact, it made taking the ride all the more important. Here was a new vision and a new community. More than a community, 'cause every great rock group is kind of like starting a religion, sort of. And Bruce surrounded himself with fellow believers. E-Street wasn't just a great rock group, or a street gang, it was a brotherhood. . . . They call him the Boss. Well, that's a bunch of crap. He works for us. More than a boss, he's the owner, because more than anyone else, Bruce Springsteen owns America's heart.[13]

The Jubilee 2000 campaign was gaining momentum and Bono appeared with Bob Geldof at the G8 Summit in Cologne, Germany, to present a petition signed by 17 million people supporting debt relief. They then met with Pope John Paul II who put on Bono's shades for a photo-op. The band could see that Bono was completely devoted to the cause and they gave him a long leash to pursue it. He and Ali celebrated the birth of their third child, their first boy, Elijah Bob Patricius Guggi Q, on August 17, 1999. Bono was also collaborating with Wyclef Jean from the Fugees, writing "New Day," and recorded a video for NetAid, an antipoverty organization. Later in the fall, concerts were held in New York, London, and Geneva to launch the organization but it was poorly attended and didn't inspire much publicity.

Eno was finally losing patience and began putting pressure on the band to come together and work on the new material. Trying to work without having Bono around was anathema to the way Eno usually worked. As the new millennium dawned, plans were made to release *Hasta la Vista Baby!*, a collection of live tracks from U2's performance in Mexico on the PopMart tour as an exclusive fan-club-only album. The band was also awarded the coveted Freedom of Dublin City from the city council. One of the privileges that comes with the honor is the right to graze sheep on public land. To celebrate, Bono and Edge released a few on Stephen's Green in the middle of the city. The band also performed a brief set and learned for the first time about Burmese Human Rights advocate, Aung San Suu Kyi, winner of the 1991 Nobel Peace Prize. She was languishing under house arrest in Rangoon and soon after Bono wrote the lyrics to "Walk On" as a tribute to her.

When Bono turned 40, Ali hired a vintage plane to fly him around Europe with his closest friends, including Gavin and Guggi. He then met Nelson Mandela for the first time in Monaco. He was living the life as a true jet-setter and criticism was bubbling up that Bono was the type that could talk the talk but not walk the walk. His lifestyle seemed at odds with his advocacy work. U2 also seemed to be losing popularity and becoming out of touch with the shifting currents of the music industry. *Pop* may not have been a commercial flop, but it was generally regarded as a middle-of-the-road album. At the same time newer bands like Radiohead were staking out fresh territory and had become the critics' darlings. Something had to be done to recapture the magic and sizzle U2 had enjoyed just a few years previously. Bono's passion for social issues had recently been reignited and he was invested in a way he hadn't been for years in focusing on making a difference in the world. He had also been thinking about death and contemplating life without his father. It was time to return to the basics and address the fundamentals.

The band finally gathered together in the studio with the same intent and awareness of what was at stake. Edge pulled out his old Gibson Explorer, the one he had bought in New York back in 1978, and wrote the opening riff for "Beautiful Day." Bono rolled his eyes at first and was reluctant to use it, but as the rest of the band kicked in he couldn't deny its infectious groove. He started working in lyrics and was sitting in the studio surrounded by the mix when he blurted out, "It's a

Nigerian president Olusegun Obasanjo, left, former United Nations secretary general Kofi Annan, center, and Bono, display a banner representing a petition signed by some 21 million people urging world leaders of the Group of Eight nations to cancel global debt, during the United Nations Millennium Summit on September 7, 2000. (AP Photo/Marty Lederhandler, File)

beautiful day!" It stuck and he worked on the rest of lyrics. "Stuck in a Moment You Can't Get Out Of" was based on the death of Michael Hutchence and Bono wrote the first draft in the heat of frustration after hearing the news:

> The greatest respect I could pay him was not to write some stupid, sentimental, soppy f***ing song. But it's sort of a declaration of your own position: it's got that attitude of, you know, when your jaw sticks out, like you do before a row. It's like somebody's in a stupor and you're trying to wake them up, 'cause the cops are coming, and they're sitting at the wheel and you're trying to get them out of the car cause they're gonna crash it. I wondered why the first verse was so first person? Why was it about me when I was writing a song about a mate? And I realised it was a defense because I felt so guilty.[14]

Edge had come up with a piano melody with a gospel feel that was reminiscent of some of Van Morrison's music. They thought about using a choir, but then settled for their own four-piece version of Edge, Bono, Eno, and Lanois. "Kite" was written for Bono's father, who had been suffering from cancer and had lost his faith: "The spiritual journey was interesting to him. Because he wasn't a believer; he didn't believe in God towards the end. He was a Catholic, but he lost his faith along the way."[15]

The album title, *All That You Can't Leave Behind,* was taken from "Walk On," Bono's tribute to Aung San Suu Kyi. She was to become a symbol for U2's commitment to human rights, her image appearing at concerts and in U2's news updates throughout the coming decade, until she was eventually freed from house arrest in 2010. The black-and-white cover image was taken in Paris's Charles de Gaulle Airport and it was Bono's idea to include the biblical reference "J33.3" on the digital clock. It refers to Jeremiah 33:3, which reads, "Call unto Me and I will answer you," which Bono referred to as "God's telephone number."[16]

The video for the first single, "Beautiful Day," was shot on the runway at the Charles de Gaulle Airport and features a plane blasting above the band as the song takes flight. The album was released on Larry's birthday, October 31, 2000, and went straight to number 1 in 32 countries but was held off in the United States by Jay-Z's *Roc La Familia*. A few weeks later, on November 13, Bob celebrated his 75th birthday at the Clarence Hotel with posters bearing his photograph and the headline, "Still Rocking at 75."[17]

The band knew they would have their work cut out for them and were prepared to work tirelessly to make the album a success. Bono said,

> I feel like I've been wearing a bowler hat and carrying a briefcase. Now I've found my voice again, and it's an amazing feeling. I've never really felt like a singer. It was always difficult for me to hear my voice on the radio. It felt tight, constricted. But at least I always had it live. But I was having a lot of difficulty on the last tour. Everyone was saying it was my lifestyle, on the phone all the time, never going to bed, smoking, drinking too much, so I was making changes but I was just not able to really get there.[18]

They immediately embarked on a six-week promotional tour that took them everywhere from London to Rio. They then played *Saturday Night Live* for the first time in their career, performing "Beautiful Day" and "Elevation." Joey Ramone stopped by and Bono name-checked the veteran punker in his performance as well as the Beatles' "All You Need is Love." The Ramones had been a lifelong inspiration and Joey was also suffering from cancer.

NOTES

1. *U2 by U2* (New York: HarperCollins, 2006), 266.

2. Tony Clayton-Lea, *U2 Popaganda: Essential U2 Quotations* (Dublin: Hodder Headline Ireland, 2007), 91.

3. *Pop*, U2.com, 1997, http://www.u2.com/discography/index/album/albumId/4011/tagName/studio_albums.

4. Clayton-Lea, *U2 Popaganda*, 63.

5. "Paul McGuinness on MSN," U2 Station, September 22, 1997, http://www.u2station.com/news/1997/09/paul-mcguinness-on-msn.php.

6. "U2's Top Ten Classic Live Songs," atU2.com, August 15, 2002, http://www.atu2.com/news/u2s-top-ten-classic-live-songs.html.

7. Matt McGee, *U2: A Diary* (London: Omnibus Press, 2008), 203.

8. "U2 Spirit in the Cathedral," U2 Station, Michael Dwyer, February 17, 1998, http://www.u2station.com/tours/1998/02/february-17–1998—perth-western-australia-australia—burswood-dome.php.

9. Ibid.

10. Michka Assayas, *Bono on Bono* (London: Hodder & Stoughton, 2005), 172–173.

11. McGee, *U2*, 208.

12. "Where Two Roads Meet—*The Million Dollar Hotel* and *All That You Can't Leave Behind*," U2faqs.com, http://www.u2faqs.com/history/f.html.

13. "Bono on Bruce Springsteen," Rock and Roll Hall of Fame Museum, http://rockhall.com/inductees/bruce-springsteen/transcript/bono-on-bruce-springsteen.

14. "Confessions of a Rock Star," atU2.com, December 15, 2000, http://www.atu2.com/news/confessions-of-a-rock-star.html.

15. Assayas, *Bono on Bono*, 24.

16. *U2 by U2*, 303.

17. "Bono's Dad Still Rocking at 75," Showbiz.ie, November 13, 2000, http://www.showbiz.ie/news/november00/13-u214.shtml.

18. "Confessions of a Rock Star.".

Chapter 8

GOODNESS IN EVERYTHING: BACK TO BASICS (2001–2005)

After Christmas, U2 won three Grammys for *All That You Can't Leave Behind* and then took off on their "Elevation" world tour choosing this time to stick with auditoriums rather than stadium-sized venues. PopMart represented the antithesis of what they were aiming for this time around and everything was on a smaller, more human scale. The band's outfits were casual T-shirts, leather jackets, and jeans while shows were stripped of anything that could be construed as a gimmick. No more giant lemons or bubble pants and Willie Williams brought it back to basics with a heart-shaped stage design, a perfect embodiment of the open-hearted themes running through the album. It was a refreshing change for the band, and Bono felt liberated from trying to outdo himself night after night. He used the space to run around the perimeter: "I really believe it is my job to attack the distance between performer and audience, from climbing speaker stacks to stage diving, it is all the same thought."[1]

Bono and Ali's fourth child, John Abraham, was born May 20, 2001, just after Bono's 41st birthday. He spoke about how being a parent had influenced his views about the world:

Well, people, I think, probably felt that having children would chill me out, but rather the opposite. It's made me a lot more interested in the world, the way it is shaped and formed, the world that they're about to enter into. And it made me more interested in politics for that reason. And I'm less patient with the process of politics and in sort of correcting the mistakes we've made over the last years in the world. And in all, it's made me a pain in the ass.

But then you understand from the feelings that you have for your children, you understand actually why wars are fought. You understand all of these terrible things. It brings—it's not all wine and roses, you know. It's—there's an acrid and bitter part, I think, to—for me, when you realize that you—you know, and I'm a—I was a complete and utter pacifist, until I had children and realized that if somebody tried to take them out of my hands.[2]

Soon after, Bono learned that his father was dying from cancer. He had been sick for a long time and was weaker and only a shadow of what he had once been. Bono was in the middle of a world tour and had huge commitments to fulfill. He discovered a form of therapy on the stage, using his lyrics and the power of the songs to imagine a conversation with his father. It was moving to witness and on some nights, overwhelming. When the tour moved to Europe Bono started flying home to Dublin regularly to be with Bob, who was now also suffering from Parkinson's disease and not able to speak much. Bono would read him Shakespeare and it reminded Bono of his mother's death. Feelings he thought he had forgotten came flooding back.

In July, Bono showed up at the G8 Summit in Genoa, Italy, to push leaders on debt relief and aid. Violence broke out on the streets and Bono condemned it but admitted he understood the reasons for it. Bob soon took a turn for the worse and Bono flew to be at his side, staying up through the night. In the morning of August 21, 2001, Bob Hewson passed away after telling a nurse to f*** off for asking him if he needed anything.[3] The same day, U2 was playing at London's Earl Court and Bono summoned all his strength to perform. In his father's memory he knelt, made a sign of the cross, and explained that "Kite" was for written for his father. While singing, he substituted "the last of the opera stars" for "rock stars" in his father's memory.

Bono took a day off after the funeral and U2 took the stage at Slane Castle on August 25. During "One," images of Bob were shown on the screen as Bono sang a few lines from the Three Degrees' "When Will I See You Again." It was incredibly moving and also a very public way to grieve. Bono felt comfortable surrounded by U2, the music, and all the fans who had come to the show.

A few weeks later, U2 took a break and Bono traveled to Bali, Indonesia, to help himself put things into perspective and deal with the death of his father. He was there with Simon Carmody, an old friend from the Lypton Village days. Carmody had been part the Golden Horde, a band that U2 had signed in 1991 to their Mother Records label. Bono ended up drinking too much but was able to write the lyrics for "One Step Closer" and "Electrical Storm." He also got the idea to cover Marvin Gaye's "What's Going On" as a charity single to benefit AIDS programs in Africa and other areas while also keeping the issue of African debt relief in the media. The project became Artists against AIDS Worldwide and included Britney Spears, Nas, Jennifer Lopez, and Destiny's Child, and also Gaye's own daughter, Nona. It was recorded in early September and Bono traveled to Venice to take some more time off and be with his family. He walked into a hotel on September 11 and saw that the World Trade Center in New York City had been hit by two passenger jets. The single was put on hold and was eventually released at the end of October with some proceeds also going to the American Red Cross to support their work in the wake of 9/11.

The tragedy of 9/11 changed the United States dramatically. People were reaching out for anything that alleviated the horror of the attacks and the music of U2 provided basic sustenance for many. With a heroic song of affirmation—"Beautiful Day"—as its kickoff, and its themes of struggle and empowerment, *All That You Can't Leave Behind* seemed tailored for the moment. The album's sales picked up and it began to get renewed airplay. U2 appeared on the telethon, *America: A Tribute to Heroes,* 10 days after the attacks, performing "Peace On Earth/Walk On" from London with Dave Stewart and Natalie Imbruglia. The band then played their first New York City concert following 9/11 on October 24 and they had planned something special. During "Walk On," a name list of those who perished in the attacks scrolled down a video screen. When the house lights were turned on during "Where the Streets Have No Name," Bono thought the entire audience had tears in their eyes: "These people were not statistics. We used these giant screens to project the names of everyone who'd lost their life. Everybody in Madison Square Garden could see somebody they knew or somebody who knew somebody, and the whole place wept."[4]

When the tour ended on December 2 Bono went home to Dublin. He was in contact with Bill and Melinda Gates about the formation of a new organization to support debt relief called DATA (Debt, Aid, Trade for Africa). In early 2002, Bono attended the World Economic Forum in New York and spoke emphatically on African issues. U2 then came together at the first Super Bowl following 9/11 in New Orleans for a 15-minute performance and then won four Grammys, including Best Rock Album and Best Song for "Walk On." Bono said, "It was like taking a big bite out of a giant apple pie. To feel the full embrace of America was the pinnacle."[5] The same month Bono was featured on the cover of *Time* magazine with the accompanying headline, "Can Bono Save the World?" The article focused on his charity work and concluded:

> At 41, Bono says, he has given up on music as a political force. He believes his work negotiating in political back rooms is more vital and effective than singing in sold-out stadiums. . . . Music does make a difference in one way; it sways people emotionally. But for Bono that is no longer enough: "When you sing, you make people vulnerable to change in their lives. You make yourself vulnerable to change in your life. But in the end, you've got to become the change you want to see in the world. I'm actually not a very good example of that—I'm too selfish, and the right to be ridiculous is something I hold too dear—but still, I know it's true."[6]

At Easter, Bono was in the south of France, near his home in Eze, when he stepped into a small church and experienced a profound sensation: "In this little church, on Easter morning, I just got down on my knees, and I let go of whatever anger I had against my father. And I thanked God for him being my father, and for the gifts that I have been given through him. And I let go of that. I wept, and I felt rid of it."[7]

The tour left Bono feeling inspired and energized in a way he hadn't felt in a long time. For the first time in years, it felt as though U2 was politically relevant and was making a real contribution to the culture. He discussed it with the rest of the band and they too felt the same way. They decided to rent a rehearsal space in Monte Carlo and went to work on new material, including "The Hands That Built America" for Martin Scorsese's new film, *Gangs of New York*.

Bono had a chance to meet President George W. Bush at the White House to discuss fighting poverty in Africa. The two appeared together on the front lawn and President Bush announced a $5 billion initiative. It was much more than Bono had anticipated and he was visibly pleased, flashing a V sign for victory or peace as he and Bush strolled across the White House lawn. It was an image that became iconic and suggested that Bono was a supporter of the administration. He wasn't, but the two men shared the same faith and bonded by discussing scripture. Bono was careful not to overtly criticize Bush. At the time the president was still quite popular and the United States was seen as fighting a justifiable war in Afghanistan. The war in Iraq wouldn't come into focus for another year to change perceptions and Bono was acting like a consummate lobbyist.

A few months later, in May, Bono left on an 11-day tour of Africa with U.S. Treasury Secretary Paul O'Neill. Everywhere the two went Bono pressured O'Neill for more U.S. aid, and it eventually paid off when Bush announced $15 billion over 15 years to fight AIDS in Africa in the 2003 State of the Union address.

In the summer of 2002, U2 finished a new song, "Electrical Storm," with Eno's protégé, William Orbit. Bono said the lyrics expressed the sense of foreboding and uncertainty that he had experienced in the United States in the aftermath of 9/11. The video was then shot in Eze to promote U2's next album, *Best of 1990–2000*, scheduled to be released in the fall. Bono then put on his best clothes to play the part of Edge's best man at his wedding to longtime girlfriend, Morleigh. The next month, Bono returned to the United States and joined the Rolling Stones onstage in Chicago before appearing on the *Oprah Winfrey Show* to promote debt relief for Africa:

Paul O'Neill, great man and a great man to hang out with, believe it or not as buttoned-up as he is, but he's Mr. Moneybags.

But he can't do anything unless the American people give him permission to spend that money. That is honestly why I'm on the program because I know you've got the budget, you've got the deficit, you've got all these elections, people are worrying about their mortgage. You have to send them the message that this is important to you, that this is about the idea of America.[8]

In October, the band received a thrill when Ireland decided to release a U2 postage stamp as part of their Irish Rock Legends series. A few months later, after the release of the *Best of U2: 1990–2000*, Bono was honored by the Simon Wiesenthal Center for "fulfilling the prophetic vision of *tikkun olam*—to help repair the world and leave it in better condition than when we found it."[9]

Bono was also collaborating with Dave Stewart from the Eurythmics and Joe Strummer on "46664 (Long Walk to Freedom)," a tribute song for the upcoming Nelson Mandela concert to be held in November. Edge and Bono ended up flying to Cape Town to perform as a duo on "One" and "Unchained Melody" in tribute to Mandela. Bono was excited about working with Joe Strummer, one of his earliest inspira-

Bono and his wife, Ali, arrive at the inaugural Love Rocks concert, February 14, 2002, in the Hollywood section of Los Angeles. (AP Photo/Chris Weeks)

tions, when news came just before Christmas that Joe had died of a heart attack. It was completely unexpected and Bono was devastated along with the rest of the rock community. The Clash and Joe's lyrics in particular had been a seminal influence on U2 and Bono said, "The Clash was the greatest rock band. They wrote the rule book for U2."[10]

Every year before the Grammy Awards the organization MusiCares chooses a musician to honor for their musical achievements and for their dedication to philanthropy. Recipients included Stevie Wonder and Sting, and in 2003 it was Bono. In an interview with *Grammy* magazine he said,

> I think I want to change the world, and I want to have fun. I don't know anyone who doesn't, by the way. Those two instincts shouldn't be mutually exclusive. Sometimes when you succeed in one area of your life, like music, you think you can apply that same momentum to other things. I suppose that's what I thought. Everything is analogous, in a way. The music industry is not that difficult to figure out. It's not rocket science. Neither is economics, as it turns out. And neither is an understanding of what is wrong with the body politic at the moment. I think it's clear we're at a real impasse.[11]

It was a star-studded event and included David Bowie, Elvis Costello, Aretha Franklin, and Bill Clinton. Later in the same month Bono was awarded another tribute—this time from the French government when he was awarded the Chevalier of Legion of Honor, France's highest civilian award.

The U.S. invasion of Iraq in March 2003 was building up at this time and the connections Bono had forged with President Bush and Britain's Tony Blair were becoming toxic. He knew he would have to tread very carefully to avoid looking as though he supported any military intervention. After a meeting with Chirac, who was also opposed to the invasion, Bono expressed his personal beliefs: "Tony Blair is not going to war for oil. Tony Blair is sincere in his convictions about Iraq. In my opinion he is sincerely wrong."[12] It complicated Bono's work, but he had friends inside and outside of government who could still help him pursue his agenda for debt relief and funding for AIDS research.

Bono creating paintings for Peter and the Wolf, *which fetched $368,000 at Christie's auction house in New York in support of the Irish Hospice Foundation, 2003. (PRNewsFoto/The Irish Hospice Foundation)*

Edge had been working on new material during this time and Bono loved what he was hearing. The songs were raw and didn't shy away from any U2isms, following a similar pattern as their previous album. When the band convened to discuss the vision for the next release they all agreed that the formula used on *All That You Can't Leave Behind*, with the four of them together bashing out the songs, was worth sticking to, but they also wanted the new album to include more guitar-driven rockers. They decided to contact legendary producer Chris Thomas and he agreed to come out to Dublin. After a promising start, things began to drag on and were looking uncertain, but by the summer they had an album's worth of material. Bono was ready to release it and was eager to begin touring again, but the rest of the band resisted.

Bono flew to Italy for Pavarotti's charity concert in May and joined the tenor on a version of "Ave Marie," adding new lyrics he had written for the occasion:

And strength is not without humility
It's weakness, an untreatable disease
And war is always the choice
Of the chosen who will not have to fight[13]

Later that same year, Bono attended Pavarotti's wedding and dedicated "All I Want Is You" to the newlyweds, adding the lyrics, "When the pasta has run dry / And the wine no longer gets you high / All I want is you."[14]

After a break, U2 flew to London's Air Studios in October to pick up recording with Thomas again, but it convinced the band that they couldn't go on. Thomas had hired a 50-piece orchestra and nothing was working right; they could tell by the looks on the faces of the orchestra members that something was very wrong. U2 decided that a trusted second opinion was needed.

In January 2004, old friend Steve Lillywhite was invited to Dublin to listen to the sessions and he felt the songs were good but knew U2 could do much better. He also knew the fans would see it that way too. Lillywhite ended up staying six months to help the band push themselves to the next level and rerecord the Thomas material. The release date was pushed into the fall as the band went to work throughout the spring and summer. The title *How to Dismantle an Atomic Bomb* seemed like an appropriate reference to the Iraq war erupting across TV and computer screens at the time, but Bono said it was about his father. The atomic bomb was his emotional connection to Bob and the dismantling was his death:

Or maybe something just lifted, like a very strange weight, and I am more at ease with myself. And this is as easy as I'll ever get, and this is pretty good. He is the atomic bomb in question and it is his era, the cold-war era, and we had a bit of a cold war, myself and him. When he died, I had no idea what would happen. I did start behaving a little odd, took on more and more projects. Looking back, now I've finally managed to say goodbye, I think that I did do some mad stuff. I got a letter from a friend of mine that said, "1) Don't leave your job, 2) your wife, 3) take large sums of money out of the bank." I wasn't doing any of that, but what he

was saying was, when fathers die, sons do mad stuff. I thought I
was ready for it.[15]

As with such a sensitive procedure, any wrong move could ignite a
catastrophe and Bono was aware that he would need to unravel his
feelings in a very cautious and caring way. When asked about how an
atomic bomb could be dismantled, Bono replied, "With love."[16]

The songs were consistent and strong throughout. "Vertigo" began as
"Native Son," a tribute to Leonard Peltier, who languishes in prison for
the death of two FBI agents he denies ever killing. It gradually moved
away from any political connotations to settle as the version Bono explained being about, "a disused soul in a well-used nightclub."[17] "Sometimes You Can't Make It on Your Own" had been around for a few years
and was the moving tune Bono sang for his father at his funeral. As
Bono said on the album's accompanying DVD, "A song can change the
world . . . it can change the temperature in the room." It went on to
win Best Song at the 2006 Grammy Awards. "Crumbs from Our Table"
was a song of disgust written against indifferent institutions that ignore
what Bono has called "stupid poverty": "'Crumbs from Your Table' is
one of the most vicious songs ever. It's full of spleen about the church
and its refusal to hear God's voice on the AIDS emergency."[18]

The cover shot of the band was done by Anton Corbijn in Portugal. The red-and-white danger motif was chosen to reflect the album's
themes of desperation and risk taking. Bono accompanied Corbijn to
his exhibition in the Netherlands called *U2 and I: The Photographs,
1982–2004*. While wandering around the exhibit, he was confronted
with one image of himself at age 21 and was struck by his expression:
"I realized how much I'd lost. I'm not talking about lines on my face
or thicker head of hair but that way of looking at the world. There was
such clarity to it, but it was so defiant in a way."[19]

The album was finally finished and in the can by July. Bono was
feeling confident that the material was as good as anything U2 had
ever done. The band flew to the south of France for a photo shoot and
while there an advanced CD of the album went missing. Interpol was
contacted and an intense search took place, but it was never found.

In the United States 2004 was an election year, and incumbent
President Bush was up for reelection against Democrat challenger John

Kerry. Bono attended both Democratic and Republican conventions so as not to appear partisan and to keep his options open for whoever might win in the November election. Back in Britain, however, he attended the Labour convention of Tony Blair, but not the one for the Conservative Party.

U2 was aware that the music industry was changing and the rise of online file sharing sites like LimeWire and the creation of Apple's iTunes were changing how music was sold and how people were listening to it. U2 had had a relationship with Apple since 2002 and they were now about to engage in a new one to promote the album along with Apple's iPod and iTunes. Two commercials were developed using the band and the single "Vertigo." They were released in October to generate publicity in the weeks before the album appeared.

How to Dismantle an Atomic Bomb was released on November 22 and became U2's fastest-selling CD ever. Rolling Stone gave it 4 out of 5 stars and on the day it appeared the band showed up on a flatbed truck performing "All Because of You" through the streets of Manhattan. In the afternoon, they played a 45-minute free concert in Brooklyn. Everything seemed to be falling into place.

The winter of 2004 was to be the 20th anniversary of *Band Aid*'s hit, "Do They Know It's Christmas?" Bono hadn't thought much about it until Bob Geldof called to tell him he was reassembling a new lineup of pop stars to record the song again for charity. Bono, George Michael, and Paul McCartney were the only original members from 1984 who joined newer celebrities like Chris Martin and Dido for *Band Aid 20*. When the single was released on November 29, it became the United Kingdom's biggest seller of 2004 as well as staying at number 1 for four weeks, just one week shorter than the original had done in 1984.

The Vertigo tour was set to begin in the New Year, but Edge's seven-year-old daughter, Sian, was diagnosed with leukemia and the tour had to be pushed forward a month. Edge found a specialist to treat her and was then able to commit to a yearlong tour. In February, the band assembled in Vancouver to rehearse and prepare.

At this time, the *Los Angeles Times* wrote an editorial supporting Bono for World Bank president:

Bono led the Drop the Debt campaign in 2000, seeking to forgive billions in loans to the Third World, and in 2002 he co-founded Debt, AIDS and Trade in Africa, a serious group that seeks to raise awareness of Africa's problems and lobby governments to help solve them. It could hardly ask for a better spokesman than its founder, whose fame has helped open doors that other lobbyists spend decades trying to crack.

Bono could enhance the World Bank's image and sell its poverty-reduction mission far more effectively than the other deserving candidates being mentioned for the job, which traditionally goes to an American—a tradition that deserves to be broken, even if not in favor of the Irish rock star.

For one thing, Bono could mobilize public opinion in favor of getting rich nations to abide by their commitments to development aid, which they rarely meet.[20]

It came as a surprise to Bono who never had any intention of heading the World Bank. He shrugged it off and appeared at the Grammys singing the Beatles' "Across the Universe" in memory of the 200,000 people who had died in the Indian Ocean tsunami. U2 won three awards, including Best Rock Song for "Vertigo." A few nights later, Bruce Springsteen inducted the band into the Rock and Roll Hall of Fame at New York's Waldorf Astoria Hotel:

Uno, dos, tres, catorce. That translates as one, two, three, fourteen. That is the correct math for a rock and roll band. For in art and love and rock and roll, the whole had better equal much more than the sum of its parts, or else you're just rubbing two sticks together searching for fire. A great rock band searches for the same kind of combustible force that fueled the expansion of the universe after the big bang. You want the earth to shake and spit fire. You want the sky to split apart and for God to pour out.

It's embarrassing to want so much, and to expect so much from music, except sometimes it happens—the Sun Sessions, Highway 61, Sgt. Peppers, the Band, Robert Johnson, Exile on Main Street, Born to Run—whoops, I meant to leave that one out (laughter)—the Sex Pistols, Aretha Franklin, the Clash, James Brown . . . the proud and public enemies it takes a nation of millions to hold back. This is music meant to take on not only the powers that be, but on a good day, the universe and God himself—if he was listening. It's man's accountability, and U2 belongs on this list.[21]

The set design for the Vertigo tour was designed once again by Willie Williams and was similar to the Elevation tour in its simplicity. Some of the main elements involved an ellipse-shaped ramp similar to the heart-shaped ramp used on the previous tour. The band took to calling the inside area of the ellipse the "bomb shelter" in reference to the title *How to Dismantle an Atomic Bomb*. U2 had left behind the big tropes of the nineties for the big social issues of the naughties and the fans were delighted. Bono wanted to display Polish artist Piotr Mlodozeniec's COEXIST symbol that made use of the Islamic crescent for the "C," the Jewish Star of David for "X," and the Christian cross for the "T." Catherine Owen, the multimedia artist who had designed the name scroll for the 9/11 victims on the previous tour, was working on a way to incorporate the Universal Declaration of Human Rights into the stage set.

As the tour wound its way through North America, Bono got word that the next G8 Summit was to be in Gleneagles, Scotland. He believed that the attending countries might actually make a substantial move to reduce the debt of the developing world and came up with the idea to hold a concert on the doorstep of the conference. He wanted to help focus the eyes of the world on the G8 Summit and he contacted Bob Geldof to see if he might be interested in helping out. Actually, Bono wanted to hold another Live Aid concert, but Geldof had stood firm against the idea for years. Then after much prodding, Geldof relented and an announcement was made at the end of May that Live 8 would be held on July 2, only six weeks away. As U2 headed to Europe in June, plans were coming together for Live 8. Ten concerts were scheduled in all the G8 countries, with the first to be held in Japan, and would include the Who, Madonna, REM, the Killers, and Youssou N'Dour.

U2 kicked off Live 8 in London's Hyde Park along with Paul McCartney playing "Sergeant Pepper's Lonely Hearts Club Band" followed by "Beautiful Day," "Vertigo," and "One." After finishing their brief set, they had to fly immediately to Vienna for an already scheduled gig, and then continued across Eastern Europe. A few days later on July 7, the London bombings occurred and Bono dedicated "Running to Stand Still" to the victims and their families.

The tour was going very well and the band returned to North America in September to begin the third leg. Bono wrote an essay, "This Generation's Moon Shot," for a November issue of *Time* magazine:

> I was a 9-year-old boy in Dublin when a man first walked on the moon. It wasn't just any man—it was an American. I thought I already knew something about America from Elvis, the movies and the hip gear sent home by Irish people who crossed the Atlantic. But now American meant something new. It meant having a sense of infinite possibility, doing the things everyone says can't be done. Even this freckle-faced Irish kid could see that America went to the moon not just because it was a scientific milestone—a career move for the human race—but because it was an adventure. . . .
>
> Beating AIDS and extreme, stupid poverty, this is our moon shot. This is our civil rights struggle, our anti-apartheid movement. This is what the history books will remember our generation for—or blame us for, if we fail.[22]

The Vertigo tour ended in December and the band returned to Dublin for the holidays. Bono soon received some astonishing news—he and Bill and Melinda Gates had been chosen as *Time*'s 2005 Persons of the Year.

NOTES

1. *U2 by U2* (New York: HarperCollins, 2006), 305.

2. "Interview with Bono," CNN, December 1, 2002, http://archives. cnn.com/TRANSCRIPTS/0212/01/lklw.00.html.

3. *U2 by U2*, 307.

4. Michka Assayas, *Bono on Bono* (London: Hodder & Stoughton, 2005), 196.

5. "Bono's World," *People*, March 4, 2002, http://www.people.com/people/archive/article/0,,20136496,00.html.

6. "Bono," *Time*, March 4, 2002, http://www.time.com/time/maga zine/article/0,9171,1001931–1,00.html.

7. Assayas, *Bono on Bono*, 23.

8. "Bono on Oprah—Part 6—2002, Sept. 20," YouTube, October 31, 2009, http://www.youtube.com/watch?v=Zjd85QwBBpc&feature= related.

9. "'Beautiful Day' for Bono," atU2.com, November 22, 2002, http://www.atu2.com/news/beautiful-day-for-bono.html.

10. "Clash Star Strummer Dies," BBC News, December 27, 2002, http://news.bbc.co.uk/2/hi/2600669.stm.

11. "Bono Honoured as 2003 MusiCares Person of the Year," atU2. com, February 20, 2003, http://www.atu2.com/news/bono-honoured-as-2003-musicares-person-of-the-year.html.

12. "Blair 'Sincerely Wrong' on Iraq—U2's Bono," atU2.com, February 28, 2003, http://www.atu2.com/news/blair-sincerely-wrong-on-iraq-u2s-bono.html.

13. Matt McGee, *U2: A Diary* (London: Omnibus Press, 2008), 258.

14. Ibid., 263.

15. "U2 Interview: Group Therapy," U2 Interviews, November 7, 2004, www.u2_interviews.tripod.com: http://u2_interviews.tripod.com/id193.html.

16. "Did U2 Plan to Dismantle an Atomic Bomb?" atU2.com, July 12, 2004, http://www.atu2.com/news/did-u2-plan-to-dismantle-an-atomic-bomb.html.

17. Niall Stokes, *U2: Into the Heart* (London: Carlton Books, 2005), 171.

18. *U2 by U2*, 324.

19. Ibid., 322.

20. "Bono for the World Bank," *LA Times*, February 25, 2005, http://articles.latimes.com/2005/feb/25/opinion/ed-bono25.

21. "Bruce Springsteen Inducts U2 into the Rock and Roll Hall of Fame," U2 Station, March 17, 2005, http://www.u2station.com/news/archives/2005/03/transcript_bruc.php.

22. "This Generation's Moon Shoot," *Time*, November 1, 2005, www.time.com: http://www.time.com/time/magazine/article/0,9171, 1124333,00.html.

Chapter 9

THE SONGS ARE IN YOUR EYES: MIDLIFE GROOVE (2006–2009)

Being named Person of the Year helped keep Bono and DATA in the headlines, and in February 2006 he gave a speech at the National Prayer Breakfast with President Bush in attendance. He spoke about debt relief:

> Preventing the poorest of the poor from selling their products while we sing the virtues of the free market, that's not charity: That's a justice issue. Holding children to ransom for the debts of their grandparents, that's not charity: That's a justice issue. Withholding lifesaving medicines out of deference to the Office of Patents, well that's not charity. To me that's a justice issue.[1]

Bono has always been a gifted communicator and knows his audience. At the Prayer Breakfast, he knew that the people in the room had the power to address the patent problem, which was making it too expensive for developing countries to reproduce or purchase the medicines needed to combat AIDS and other deadly diseases. His speech helped raise the issue in the headlines worldwide.

A few weeks later, U2 gathered at the Grammys to pick up five more awards including Album and Song of the Year just as the band was getting ready to kick off the South American leg of the Vertigo tour in Monterrey, Mexico. When the band arrived in Chile, Bono was presented with the Pablo Neruda Merit Award, the country's highest honor for the arts. In the middle of the tour, Bono appeared via video link at the *New Musical Express* awards to give his old friend, Bob Geldof, a tribute as the magazine's Hero of the Year. Although nine years older, Geldof was Bono's partner in music and politics and shared a passion for helping Africa. Geldof had a reputation for speaking his mind and using harsh language without regard for who might be listening. Bono took advantage of this in his tribute:

> I'm so very pleased that upon asking Bob to do Live 8, we did not listen when he told us to f*** off. And I hope he is too. Because a cheque worth 50 billion dollars has been signed for the poorest people on the planet. Every time somebody buys one of these Live 8 DVDs we'll put pressure on the politicians to cash the cheque. Thank you very much for this award. And to my friend who is picking it up in all our honor: F***. Off.[2]

When the South American tour finished in Argentina, Bono flew with his family to Australia for a break before resuming the last leg of the tour down under. He then got the bad news that Edge's daughter had taken a turn for the worse and U2 would have to postpone the tour until November. Bono popped up at the Samuel Beckett Centenary Festival in Dublin and recalled the time he met the author and presented him with a copy of *The Unforgettable Fire*. But he was never sure if Beckett had ever given it a listen.

The FIFA World Cup, scheduled for June in Germany, was just around the corner and U2 had agreed to record some commercials with the ESPN network. The theme was "One Game Changes Everything" and Bono's ad about the Ivory Coast included his voice-over:

> It's a simple thing. Just a ball and a goal. That simple thing . . . closes the schools, closes the shops, closes a city and stops a war. After three years of civil war, feuding factions talked for the first

time in years and the president called a truce because the Ivory Coast qualified for its first-ever World Cup.[3]

Bono was invited to edit the *Independent* newspaper in dedicating an entire issue to AIDS awareness. He enlisted the help of artist Damien Hirst to design the cover, which announced, "No News Today: Just 6,500 Africans died today as the result of a preventable, treatable disease. (HIV/AIDS)." Half the funds raised went to the Global Fund to Fight AIDS. Shortly after this, Bono went on a 10-day tour of Africa as a representative of DATA.

U2 had always been shrewd investors and big spenders. Their tours often began in the red and eventually took some time before they reached the black, but by the end they were usually among the highest-grossing musical acts in the world. The band was eager to find lucrative investments and sought to build an apartment complex in Dublin's south docklands. They also made the controversial decision to move their royalties to the Netherlands to avoid paying Irish taxes. The band began to attract some very harsh criticism for this move, as did Bono when he bought a stake in *Forbes*, the elite business magazine. These decisions were beginning to cause a backlash and some accused the band and Bono of hypocrisy, of campaigning for the eradication of poverty while rolling in cash. Bono usually dismissed the hectoring as whining from outside the mainstream of public opinion, but some of the critiques were beginning to resonate and spread further.

In September, U2 joined Green Day in Abbey Road Studios to cut a few tracks for the upcoming NFL performance celebrating the reopening of the New Orleans Superdome in the wake of Hurricane Katrina. They had chosen "The Saints Are Coming" by Stuart Adamson's first band, the Skids, and asked producer Rick Rubin to helm the controls. U2 had been considering Rubin for their next album and Rubin had a reputation for excellence, working on critically acclaimed albums by artists as diverse as the Red Hot Chili Peppers and Johnny Cash. The sessions went off well and the performance attracted a television audience of 15 million, making it the second most watched cable broadcast ever. The song was later included on *U218 Singles*, released in November.

Bono was getting involved with bridging the divide between commerce and charity. He joined Ali in 2005 to launch EDUN, a fashion brand with a mission to encourage trade with Africa and promote the continent as a viable location to do business. In October, he appeared with Oprah in Chicago promoting PRODUCT (RED), a brand he founded with Bobby Shriver to help companies participate in the Global Fund to Fight AIDS, Tuberculosis, and Malaria, started by Bill Gates in 2002. The initiative received some criticism when a group of San Francisco artists put together www.buylesscrap.org targeting the campaign for suggesting that conspicuous consumption was an answer for the world's problems.[4]

Bono then had to return to Dublin to give testimony in a trial against his former stylist, Lola Cashman. U2 alleged she had stolen some items worth $7,300 from *The Joshua Tree* tour back in 1987. She had also written a tell-all book about the band in 2003, *Inside the Zoo with U2*, which was perceived by the band as a disloyal betrayal. Throughout the time he was in the courtroom, Bono avoided eye contact with Cashman and a month later U2 won the case and Cashman was forced to return the items. She has since said, "I don't feel any animosity. To me, I was fighting corporate U2."[5]

Chelsea and Ivory Coast soccer player Didier Drogba, left, and Bono pose for a photograph at the announcement of the partnership between Nike and Red, in London, November 30, 2009. Lace Up Save Lives is a partnership to help fight HIV/AIDS in Africa. (AP Photo/Kirsty Wigglesworth)

Before their tour of Australia was about to resume, old friend and rock journalist Neil McCormick was enlisted to help edit a definitive autobiography of the band called *U2 by U2*. It was a huge coffee-table book filled with firsthand interviews and photographs spanning their entire career.

The Australian tour opened with Bono calling for the release from Guantanamo Bay of Australian David Hicks, who was being held on alleged terrorism charges. Bono was asked about his political statements: "The rock stars are all too cool. And I don't want to be that, I've gotten a bit too cool. I want to be like I was as a kid, I want to stay hot and passionate rather than cool."[6]

Bono appeared onstage with Kylie Minogue in Sydney and then the band joined Pearl Jam and local songwriting legend Paul Kelly in Melbourne for the concert Make Poverty History. U2 and Pearl Jam combined as UJAM on a cover of Neil Young's "Rockin' in the Free World." In Auckland, New Zealand, U2 performed the Greg Carroll tribute "One Tree Hill" for the first time since 1990 and joined others in calling for a tree to be replanted on top of Maungakiekie, the Maori name for the hill. When U2 arrived in Japan, Bono was asked to speak at Keio University in Tokyo and encouraged aid and engagement with Africa. The Vertigo tour wrapped up in Honolulu in December with Pearl Jam and Green Day's Billie Joe Armstrong joining U2 onstage for covers of "Rockin' in the Free World" and "The Saints Are Coming."

After taking a break for the holidays, Bono emerged to receive the Chairman's Award from The National Association for the Advancement of Colored People (NAACP) and delivered an inspiring speech:

> Well today the world looks again to the NAACP. We need the community that taught the world about civil rights to teach it something about human rights. Yeah! I'm talking about the right to live like a human, the right to live period. Those are the stakes in Africa right now. Five and a half thousand Africans dying every day of AIDS, a preventable, treatable disease. Nearly a million Africans most of them children dying every year from malaria. Death by mosquito bite. This is not about charity, as you know here in this room. This is about justice, it's about justice and equality.[7]

Perhaps no one outside of rock influenced Bono's idea of America more than Martin Luther King Jr. and the civil rights movement that the NAACP championed in the and fifties and sixties. As he said, "When people talk about the greatness of America, I just think of the NAACP." The movement represented the best of the United States for Bono. He then penned another essay in *Time* magazine, "A Time for Miracles" on the 50th anniversary of the Treaty of Rome, which had established the European Economic Community. He explained that this was a result of once-warring nations of France and Germany forgiving one another and coming together for the greater good of Europe. He used the Irish word for helping each other when times are hardest— *meitheal*—to suggest that now was the time for the richest nations to help the poorest:

> There's an Irish word, meitheal. It means that the people of the village help one another out most when the work is the hardest. Most Europeans are like that. As individual nations, we may argue over the garden fence, but when a neighbor's house goes up in flames, we pull together and put out the fire. History suggests it sometimes takes an emergency for us to draw closer. Looking inward won't cut it. As a professional navel gazer, I recommend against that form of therapy for anything other than songwriting. We discover who we are in service to one another, not the self. Today many rooms in our neighbor's house, Africa, are in flames. From the genocide in Darfur to the deathbeds in Kigali, with six AIDS patients stacked onto one cot, from the child dying of malaria to the village without clean water, conditions in Africa are an affront to every value we Europeans have ever seen fit to put on paper. We see in Somalia and Sudan what happens if more militant forces fill the void and stir dissent within what is, for the most part, a pro-Western and moderate Muslim population. (Nearly half of Africa's people are devotees of Islam.) So whether as a moral or strategic imperative, it's folly to let this fire rage.[8]

Bono had become a respected expert on issues of debt relief and aid and it was for this work, as well as for his role in U2, that he was awarded an honorary knighthood from the queen of England. His for-

mal title from that moment became Knight Commander of the Most
Excellent Order of the British Empire, or KBE for short: "You have my
permission to call me pretty much anything, Lord of Lords, your demi-
Godness, but not Sir. . . . How much do you think I'd get for this thing
in Weirs? [Dublin jewelry shop]."[9]

Bono and Edge traveled to the United States to begin working on
a dream they had shared since they wrote the music for *A Clockwork
Orange* back in the early 1990s. They signed on to do the music and lyrics for *Spiderman: The Broadway Musical*, which would eventually take
four years and countless headaches before it actually opened on Broadway. In April, *American Idol* ran a charity show and Bono appeared to
promote the ONE charity, named after U2's *Achtung Baby* song. He
then joined Laurie Anderson and David Bowie supporting Lou Reed,
who was being honored by Syracuse University, his alma mater "for
excellence in the arts."

The time had come to plan a new album. The band was pleased
with their work with Rick Rubin, but felt that his style clashed with
U2's work ethic. In May, U2 traveled to Fez, Morocco, with Brian Eno

U2, *from left, Larry Mullen Jr., Bono, The Edge, and Adam Clayton arrive at
the 60th International Film Festival in Cannes, southern France, May 20, 2007.
(AP Photo/Andrew Medichini, File)*

and Daniel Lanois once again to work on songs. They had been there before in 1991 for the video of "Mysterious Ways" and had fallen in love with the city. Bono agreed with Eno that location and surroundings played a vital role in the songwriting process: "I wait for the music to tell me what I'm going to sing. I improvise a lot, and I don't really know where we're going. It's only later that I sit down to write. It's sort of like we're on pilgrimage, barefoot, and we truly don't know where the music will take us."[10]

Bono also shared a love for Arabic music with Eno, who referred to it as "teleological." Eno was convinced that it would exert a big influence on Western pop music: "There are things I like a lot about Arabic music which are different to what we do in western music and so we have started trying to incorporate some of those elements. It is not a question of sounds so much but of different structural decisions about how things are made."[11]

The band was beginning to agree that the next album would be different from the last two. They were eager to explore bigger themes and more expansive sonic terrain than the rock orientated, guitar-based songs of *How to Dismantle an Atomic Bomb*.

U2 frontman Bono high-fives with a student before a ceremony to confer the degree of doctor of laws at Keio University in Tokyo, May 27, 2008. (AP Photo/ Itsuo Inouye)

After finishing work in Fez, Bono showed up at the TEDGlobal 2007 conference in Tanzania. He had won the TED Prize back in 2005 and his moving speech had contributed to the organization's focus on Africa and the idea behind this conference. He then traveled to Germany in time for the G8 Summit and paired with Bob Geldof to denounce world leaders for their hollow promises about fighting AIDS and malaria. Bono knew he had to hold the politicians accountable when they broke promises, and he rarely pulled his punches.

In July, Bono was given another opportunity to edit, this time a *Vanity Fair* issue devoted to Africa. He assembled a formidable arsenal of celebrities for the cover including George W. Bush, Desmond Tutu, Jay-Z, Oprah Winfrey, and presidential candidate Barack Obama. U2 had also donated a cover of John Lennon's "Instant Karma" to Amnesty International's compilation album to protest the ongoing genocide in Sudan's Darfur region. Bono then received some sad news about friend Luciano Pavarotti who died at the age of 70. Bono wrote, "Some can sing opera; Luciano Pavarotti was an opera. He lived the songs, his opera was a great mash of joy and sadness; surreal and earthy at the same time; a great volcano of a man who sang fire but spilled over with a love of life in all its complexity, a great and generous friend."[12]

Bono was maintaining a busy schedule, even appearing in a film inspired by the Beatles, *Across the Universe*, as Dr. Robert, singing "I Am the Walrus" and "Lucy in the Sky with Diamonds." He was then presented with the Liberty Medal by former recipient George H. W. Bush. It was an awkward ceremony that put together two men who had been on opposite ends of a parody during the Zoo Tour, but Bono laughed it off. He then struck a more serious note and took the opportunity to address the sensitive issue of torture:

Today I read in the *Economist* an article reporting that over 38 percent of Americans support some type of torture in exceptional circumstances. My country? No. Your country? Tell 'em no. Today, when you pin this great honor on me I ask you, I implore you as an Irishman who has seen some of these things close up, I ask you to remember, you do not have to become a monster to defeat a monster. Your America's better than that.[13]

Bono had learned to shape-shift and transition effortlessly from role to role. He was known as world statesman as much as a celebrity pop singer. In November, the United States elected their first black president, Barack Obama, someone Bono had already known for a few years. The Obama campaign had been using "City of Blinding Lights" as its theme song, which resonated with the "hope and change" mantra of its core message. When the band was invited to perform at Lincoln Memorial for the We Are One inauguration concert in January 2009, they performed the song along with "Pride."

At the end of the year, Bono and Edge collaborated with Grateful Dead lyricist Robert Hunter and friend Simon Carmody on "The Ballad of Ronnie Drew," a tribute to the Dubliner who had been suffering from cancer. They joined Christy Moore, Sinead O'Connor, Shane MacGowan, and others in the studio in January 2008 and released the song soon after. Bono and Carmody then collaborated on another song, "I Am the Blues," for French legend, Johnny Hallyday's album, *Le couer d'un homme* (*The Heart of a Man*).

U2 had been trying to stay ahead of the changes in the music industry and had spoken out against illegal file sharing. Paul had been more aggressive in his criticism and in his support of penalties being levied against Internet service providers (ISPs) who hosted any sites engaged in the activity. At Hong Kong's Music Matters conference in June, Paul lashed out at ISPs and was harshly critical of Radiohead and their recent decision to release *In Rainbows* through their own website. Bono later felt compelled to apologize:

> We disagree with Paul's assessment of Radiohead's release as "having backfired to a certain extent." We think they were courageous and imaginative in trying to figure out some new relationship with their audience. Such imagination and courage are in short supply right now . . . they're a sacred talent and we feel blessed to be around at the same time.[14]

Work on the new album intensified and a release date was set for October. In August, portions of it leaked onto the Net. Apparently, Bono had been caught playing it in his home in Eze and a passerby recorded it with his cell phone. At the end of the summer, progress had slowed and the release date was pushed into early 2009. "We know we have to emerge soon but we also know that people don't want another U2 album unless it is our best ever album. It has to be our most innovative, our most challenging . . . or what's the point?"[15]

In November, the band was in London doing the final mixes and speaking to the press. U2 announced the title would be *No Line on the Horizon* and the first single would be "Get on Your Boots," the fastest song the band had ever recorded. Bono cited "Moment of Surrender" as his favorite song in the album.

The album was finally scheduled for release in February 2009. A few weeks before, the single "Get on Your Boots" was unleashed with much fanfare but it only reached 37 in the U.S. charts and 12 in the U.K. charts. It was U2's worst showing since 1997. The album was also being greeted by protests organized by the Debt and Development Coalition Ireland against U2's decision to move their royalties outside of Ireland to Netherlands. The group included Concern Worldwide, Oxfam, and Trócaire. The criticism "stung" Bono who responded in the *Irish Times*:

> I can understand how people outside the country wouldn't under-
> stand how Ireland got to its prosperity but everybody in Ireland
> knows that there are some very clever people in the Government
> and in the Revenue who created a financial architecture that
> prospered the entire nation—it was a way of attracting people
> to this country who wouldn't normally do business here. What's
> actually hypocritical is the idea that then you couldn't use a fi-
> nancial services centre in Holland. The real question people need
> to ask about Ireland's tax policy is: 'Was the nation a net gain
> benefactor?' And of course it was—hugely so.[16]

The tax-evasion label was bothering U2 and was beginning to catch on. Part of the problem was that it was basically accurate—the band was being opportunistic and looking to avoid high tax rates. It wasn't against the law, others did it, but U2 wasn't supposed to be like other bands. They were supposed to be different and the decision to move their royalties to the Netherlands was for purely commercial reasons and had nothing to do with the altruism the band was known for.

No Line on the Horizon, U2's 12th studio album, was released at the end of February 2009 and debuted at number one in 30 countries. It was the band's seventh number 1 in the United States, but sales tapered off soon after. *No Line on the Horizon* was recognized as a "brave record"[17] but received mixed reviews. *Rolling Stone* gave it a rare 5 out of 5 star rating and called it their best since *Achtung Baby*,[18] while *NME* gave it 7 out of 10 saying it was "a grand, sweeping, brave record that, while not quite the reinvention they pegged it as, suggests they've got the chops to retain their relevance well into their fourth decade as a band."[19]

No Line on the Horizon shied away from big hooks and pithy statements. Expansive and meandering, the album indulged in sonic textures at the expense of melody. Lyrically, Bono addressed topics more subtly and Eno exerted more influence over the production. Bono said of Eno:

> What he's listening for is a unique feeling, a unique mood and a unique palate. And he doesn't get hits—I bet he told Coldplay to leave "Viva la Vida" off their album. Brian would listen to "(I Can't Get No) Satisfaction" and say, "I love that song, but can we get rid of the guitar bits? You know, the part that goes duhnt-duhnt-dunna dun?"[20]

One of the strongest tracks is the almost eight-minute epic "Moment of Surrender." It soon became a fan favorite and questions were raised about why it wasn't chosen as the album's first single rather than the much weaker "Get on Your Boots." The song is a midtempo, gospel-flavored reflection on the struggles of living in a fallen world, cut through with a transcendent chorus. Bono asks love "to believe in me" as he grapples with "a vision over visibility."

U2 began a worldwide promo tour that included five consecutive nights on *The David Letterman Show*. In March, it was announced that the U2 360 stadium tour of the United States would begin in the fall with a gargantuan set design including a huge structure dubbed "the Claw" that would make the stage and band visible from all sides. As set designer Willie Williams said, "Everyone who sees it says that it looks like something different. Tintin's rocket. The War of the Worlds. Cactus. Octopus. Claw. Whenever it started to look like something. . . . But it does look as though it has escaped from a giant space aquarium."[21]

As the promo tour came to an end, it was apparent that *No Line on the Horizon* was not selling as well as had hoped and expectations were high that the tour would make up for the shortfall in declining CD sales. U2 360 opened in Barcelona on June 30, with David Bowie's "Space Oddity" playing as the band mounted the stage and kicked off the tour with "Breathe." It was just days after the "King of Pop," Michael Jackson, had died. Bono dedicated "Angel of Harlem" to his memory while the band mashed together Jackson's "Man in the Mirror" with "Don't Stop 'til You Get Enough."

As the tour picked up steam, new elements were added and subtracted. The band posted a face mask of Aung San Suu Kyi on their website and asked fans to download it and put it on at the next concert in support of the Nobel Laureate. The band began dedicating "Sunday Bloody Sunday" to the people of Iran who were in the streets protesting for freedom and democracy and suffering enormously for it. The stage was flooded in the same green color that opposition candidate Mir Hossein Mousavi had used for his campaign. The poem "Song of

Bono performs during the 360 Degree Tour at the Olympic Stadium in Berlin, July 18, 2009. (AP Photo/ Gero Breloer, File)

the Reed Flute" by the 13th-century Persian Sufi Rumi was scrawled across the video screen:

> Listen to the reeds as they sway apart
> hear them speak of lost friends. .
> its song and its word break the veil . . .[22]

As the tour wound on, the band picked up momentum and received positive reviews throughout the summer and into the tour's North American kickoff in Chicago. In late September and early October, Bono appeared via video link at both British Labour and Conservative Party conferences to encourage the parties to continue supporting international aid. He said to the Tories, "Hello there, if you can swallow an Irish man saying what's great about Great Britain, indulge me for a minute. Because what's happened over the last few years in Britain's relationship with the developing world has been so inspiring to me."[23]

Bono then weighed in on Barack Obama's controversial Nobel Peace Prize addressing his critics by writing in his *New York Times* column, "America shouldn't turn up its national nose at popularity contests." He also explained why he thought Obama deserved it:

> So here's why I think the virtual Obama is the real Obama, and why I think the man might deserve the hype. It starts with a quotation from a speech he gave at the United Nations last month:
>
> "We will support the Millennium Development Goals, and approach next year's summit with a global plan to make them a reality. And we will set our sights on the eradication of extreme poverty in our time."
>
> They're not my words, they're your president's. If they're not familiar, it's because they didn't make many headlines. But for me, these 36 words are why I believe Mr. Obama could well be a force for peace and prosperity —if the words signal action.[24]

At the end of October, U2's Los Angeles concert at the Rose Bowl was streamed live on YouTube for free around the world and was the first time a show of such size was streamed live. In November, U2 released a deluxe version of *The Unforgettable Fire* and the usually critical

Pitchfork awarded it 9.3 out of 10: *"The Unforgettable Fire* isn't U2's biggest commercial success (that would be *The Joshua Tree*) or its most rewarding artistic coup (*Achtung Baby*), but without it those records would not exist. It's a transitional album of the highest magnitude."[25]

U2 experienced some embarrassment at the 2009 MTV Europe Music Awards that were celebrating the 20th anniversary of the fall of the Berlin Wall. The show was to take place in front of the Brandenburg Gate, but was surrounded by a barrier reminiscent of the Berlin Wall. The band claimed the mistake was due to the organizers of the event— MTV Europe. U2 performed six songs, including a duet with Jay-Z on "Sunday Bloody Sunday" that featured Bono attempting to rap.

At the end of the month, U2 confirmed that they would be playing at the Glastonbury Festival in 2010 for its 40th anniversary. Glaston-bury founder, Michael Eavis, said, "The 26-year-old rumour has finally come true. At last, the biggest band in the world are going to play the best festival in the world. Nothing could be better for our 40th anniversary party."[26]

U2 and Bono had been receiving more criticism for moving their royalties from Ireland to avoid taxes and calls of hypocrisy for being rich celebrities speaking about alleviating poverty were growing louder. In response Bono said,

> You can still contribute even if you are not as fortunate as I am. I've been blessed and I've been over-rewarded for what I do and I'm trying to give my time and my resources but you know, I'm a rich rock star, so shoot me. I'm having a great life and even though I can be a pain in the a** going on about all this stuff, the band feel strongly about it too.[27]

NOTES

1. "Bono: Keynote Address at the 54th National Prayer Breakfast," American Rhetoric, February 2, 2006, http://www.americanrhetoric. com/speeches/bononationalprayerbreakfast.htm.

2. "Transcript of Bono's Effing NME Award Speech," U2LOG, February 26, 2006, www.u2log.com: http://u2log.com/2006/02/26/tran script-of-bonos-effing-nme-award-speech/.

3. "U2 is Giving a Voice to ESPN's Coverage," *New York Times*, June 8, 2006, http://www.nytimes.com/2006/06/08/sports/soccer/08sandomir.html?fta=y.

4. "Costly Red Campaign Reaps Meager $18 Million," atU2.com, March 5, 2007, http://www.atu2.com/news/costly-red-campaign-reaps-meager-18-million.html.

5. "How Lola Has Survived After Battle with U2," atU2.com, January 25, 2009, http://www.atu2.com/news/how-lola-has-survived-after-battle-with-u2.html.

6. "Tour Puts Bono to the Test," atU2.com, November 3, 2006, http://www.atu2.com/news/tour-puts-bono-to-the-test.html.

7. "Bono's NAACP Chairman's Award Acceptance Speech," Independent Bloggers' Alliance, March 6, 2007, http://independent bloggers.wordpress.com/2007/03/06/bonos-naacp-chairmans-award-acceptance-speech.

8. "A Time for Miracles," *Time*, March 22, 2007, http://www.time.com/time/magazine/article/0,9171,1601932,00.html#ixzz1RtEmEBL8.

9. Tony Clayton-Lea, *U2 Popaganda: Essential U2 Quotations* (Dublin: Hodder Headline Ireland, 2007), 119.

10. "Exclusive: Bono's Pilgrimage," atU2.com, June 18, 2007, http://www.atu2.com/news/exclusive-bonos-pilgrimage.html.

11. "Songwriting in Morocco, Part 2," atU2.com, June 20, 2007, www.atu2.com:http://www.atu2.com/news/songwriting-in-morocco-pt-2.html.

12. "Bono's Tribute to Pavarotti," BBC News, September 6, 2007, http://news.bbc.co.uk/2/hi/entertainment/6981703.stm.

13. "Bono and DATA 2007," National Constitution Center, September 27, 2007, http://constitutioncenter.org/libertymedal/recipient_2007.html.

14. "U2 Defends Radiohead in Letter to *NME* Magazine," atU2.com, June 25, 2008, http://www.atu2.com/news/u2-defends-radiohead-in-letter-to-nme-magazine.html.

15. "Next U2 Album Pushed to 2009," atU2.com, September 3, 2008, http://www.atu2.com/news/next-u2-album-pushed-to-early-2009.html.

16. "Bono 'Hurt' by Criticism of U2 Move to Netherlands to Cut Tax," atU2.com, February 27, 2009, http://www.atu2.com/news/bono-hurt-by-criticism-of-u2-move-to-netherlands-to-cut-tax.html.

17. "Album Review: U2," *NME*, February 26, 2009, http://www.nme.com/reviews/u2/10149.

18. "U2: No Line on the Horizon," *Rolling Stone*, February 20, 2009, http://www.rollingstone.com/music/albumreviews/no-line-on-the-horizon-20090220.

19. "Album Review: U2," *NME*, February 26, 2009, http://www.nme.com/reviews/u2/10149.

20. "U2 Talk 'Horizon' Follow Up, Spider-Man Musical," *Rolling Stone*, March 4, 2009, http://www.rollingstone.com/music/news/u2-talk-horizon-follow-up-spider-man-musical-in-rolling-stone-cover-story-20090304.

21. "What Has 4 Legs, in the Round?" atU2.com, June 21, 2009, http://www.atu2.com/news/what-has-4-legs-in-the-round.html.

22. "Iran: U2's Green-Tinted Tributes to Iranian Protesters," *Babylon and Beyond* (blog), *LA Times*, July 10, 2009, http://latimesblogs.latimes.com/babylonbeyond/2009/07/iran-u2-tributes-iranian-protestors.html.

23. "Bono Makes Surprise Appearance at Tory Conference," atU2.com, October 8, 2009, http://www.atu2.com/news/bono-makes-surprise-appearance-at-tory-conference.html.

24. "Rebranding America," *New York Times*, October 17, 2009, http://www.nytimes.com/2009/10/18/opinion/18bono.html?pagewanted=all.

25. "U2: Unforgettable Fire," Pitchfork, November 2, 2009, http://pitchfork.com/reviews/albums/13654-the-unforgettable-fire-deluxe-edition.

26. "U2 to Headline Glastonbury 40th Anniversary," *Metro*, November 23, 2009, http://www.metro.co.uk/metrolife/775746-u2-to-headline-glastonbury-40th-anniversary.

27. "Bono: 'I'm Overpaid, So Shoot Me,'" *Telegraph*, December 2, 2009, http://www.telegraph.co.uk/news/celebritynews/6708665/Bono-Im-overpaid-so-shoot-me.html.

Chapter 10

ASCENT: NEW PROSPECTS
(2010 AND BEYOND)

Early in the New Year, Bono was interviewed by Carla Bruni-Sarkozy and he spoke about his parents' influence:

> My parents taught me to be highly suspicious of religions in all the ways they can be extreme, but also to be very reverent before the idea that Jesus Christ was born in poverty, lying on hay, and that he was at the service of the poor and the lowly. I have that reverence, and I am a believer.[1]

He also spoke about his love for Bob Dylan:

> Since I was 12 years old, when I used to listen to Bob Dylan in the '70s, stretched out on the bed in my little room on the north side of Dublin. The outside world was so depressed, but Bob Dylan was singing in my ear that the world could change. I believed him and I still believe him. . . . Dylan gives me shivers, too. And I love his later songs, the ones he wrote at 50. I love his discipline and his continuity. I'm thinking of that phrase "discipline and obedience in the same direction." . . . If could get one motto tattooed

on my arm, it would be this one: "A long obedience in the same
direction."[2]

Bono was one of rock's leading front men and in April, *Q Magazine*
listed him second of all-time behind Liam Gallagher of Oasis. He had
always displayed a respect and an understanding of his role based on his
first being a devoted fan:

> Don't imagine the audience doesn't know who you really are—
> they really do . . . in a very intimate way. You live in their ear after
> all, just next door to the brain, down the hall to the bedroom of
> their heart. Especially if they sleep with earphones. Very, very in-
> timate. They have heard the sound of your spirit snap and stretch.
> (Truth is, you probably don't know who you are.)[3]

In April, Bono and Bob Geldof edited the Canadian *Globe and Mail*
newspaper's all-Africa edition in the lead-up to June's G8/G20 conference in Toronto. The issue ran on May 10, Bono's 50th birthday. A few
weeks later, while rehearsing for the North American leg of the 360
tour in Munich, Bono fell and injured his back. He was rushed to hospital where he underwent emergency surgery, but it was too serious for
him to commit to the upcoming shows. The tour was postponed indefi-
nitely and U2's Glastonbury gig had to be canceled. The band issued
a statement promising the North American gigs would be rescheduled
for the spring/summer of 2011.

In his regular column for the *New York Times,* Bono celebrated the
release of the "Saville report," which inquired into the January 30,
1972, "Bloody Sunday" incident that inspired U2's "Sunday Bloody
Sunday." Bono referred to British prime minister David Cameron's
apology writing that "the world broke rhyme":

> It was inconceivable to many that a Tory prime minister could man-
> age to get these words out of his mouth. It was also inconceivable —
> before he uttered the carefully minted phrasing —that he would
> be listened to by a hushed crowd gathered in Guildhall Square
> in Derry, a place not famous for its love of British leaders of any
> stripe, and that he would be cheered while speaking on specially

erected screens that earlier had been used to relay images from the World Cup.

Thirty-eight years did not disappear in an 11-minute speech—how could they, no matter how eloquent or heartfelt the words? But they changed and morphed, as did David Cameron, who suddenly looked like the leader he believed he would be. From prime minister to statesman.[4]

In August, Bono had recovered enough to kick off U2's third leg of the 360 tour in Turin, Italy. They had started introducing new material like "North Star" into their set and Bono was claiming that the band had three albums of new songs ready to record if they could find the time to get into the studio.

Bono and Edge's musical, *Spider-Man: Turn Off the Dark*, was scheduled to open in December and rehearsals were in full swing by September. Bono explained to *60 Minutes*: "We've moved out of the rock and roll idiom in places, into some very new territory for us, there's big show tunes and dance songs."[5]

U2 was also preparing for the fourth leg of the tour to open in Australia in November when the Broadway production began to run into difficulties. *Spider-Man* was eventually postponed into the New Year due to recurring stage problems and injuries.

Through years of touring the United States, and through his involvement in the RED antipoverty campaign, Bono got to know and work with Bobby Shriver. Shriver is the son of Eunice Kennedy Shriver, sister of President John F. Kennedy and founder of the Special Olympics, and Sargent Shriver, renowned philanthropist and founder of the American Peace Corps. In January, Shriver passed away and Bono penned a tribute in his *New York Times* column, writing, "Robert Sargent Shriver changed the world more than a few times and, I am happy to say, changed my world forever."[6]

As U2 was preparing to perform in South Africa for the first time since 1998, accusations of discrimination were leveled at the band from the South African Roadies Association (SARA). They claimed U2 and other big acts were refusing to employ black road production crews. Paul fired back pointing out that over 95 percent of the crews were black, but that the band had offered to meet with representatives of

SARA to discuss their concerns. The sides were able to diffuse the controversy, but Bono stirred up more when he was asked to comment on
the South African song, "Shoot the Boer," aka "Shoot the Farmer." It
had become an anthem during the antiapartheid struggle in the 1980s.
South Africa's highest court was considering whether it violated the
rights of Afrikaners and should be banned as hate speech after African
National Congress youth league leader, Julius Malema, started using it
at some recent rallies. Bono said he thought it was the equivalent of
folk music: "When I was a kid and I'd sing songs I remember my uncles
singing . . . rebel songs about the early days of the Irish Republican
Army."[7]

He went on to sing a song whose lyrics spoke of carrying guns and
readying them for action. "We sang this and it's fair to say it's folk
music." However, Bono added that singing the song could only be acceptable, given the right perspective and circumstances. "Would you
want to sing that in a certain community? It's pretty dumb," he said.[8]

Problems with *Spider-Man: Turn Off the Dark* persisted, and once
again the opening was pushed forward to the early summer and director
Julie Taymor was replaced. It was costing millions and had become the
most expensive Broadway musical of all-time. Many of the problems
had to do with the script and the special effects not working properly.

U2 went on to South America and in April the 360 tour became the
highest-grossing tour of all time, surpassing the Rolling Stones' 2005–
2007, A Bigger Bang. The band was averaging $6.4 million per show
and was set to gross $700 million by the time it was to finish in July.[9]

After Osama Bin Laden was killed, Bono expressed mixed feelings:
"I don't believe it was an execution, as some have suggested. The safety
of the Navy SEALs was and should be pre-eminent. Part of me would
have liked to have seen a trial. When the allies brought Nazi war crimi-
nals to justice at Nuremberg, they showed the world that despite the
grave evil that had been done to them, they would demonstrate a very
different value system."[10]

In May, U2 were back in North America for the final leg of 360 tour,
which had been rescheduled after Bono's back injury. Bono and Edge
appeared on the *American Idol* finale in Los Angeles to perform "Rise
above 1" with Reeve Carney, the singer/actor who played Peter Parker
in *Spider-Man: Turn Off the Dark*. They had also invited director Davis

Guggenheim, who did *It Might Get Loud*, the documentary featuring Edge, Jimmy Page, and Jack White, to shoot a video about *Achtung Baby*. U2 was planning to reissue the album in the fall and wanted to record a video for it in Winnipeg's Burton Cummings Theatre.

A few weeks later, Bono was out walking with his assistant in West Vancouver when it started to rain. They started hitchhiking to Horseshoe Bay and were picked up by an NHL player for the Edmonton Oilers, Gilbert Brule. Bono was grateful and gave Brule and his girlfriend a pair of tickets and backstage passes to their show in Edmonton.[11]

When Barack Obama visited Ireland in June, Bono spoke to *Hot Press* about his admiration for the U.S. president:

> He feels like one of us that became one of them—i.e. he's recognisable as a person you might have seen at a show or sports event. He feels familiar to me, and I think that's good. Whereas Bill Clinton is a very physical person in a room, he puts his hand on your shoulder, he's a great emotional arm-wrestler, Barack Obama has the demeanour of one you would play chess with. And then, of course, his secret weapon is his flash of a smile and a wicked sense of humour. He's very funny. You don't expect that from the chess player and that's his charm, and it is literally a winning smile because it's hard to stand up to—because it isn't insincere. A lot of politicians need to control their smile, it's like you can see the wires (laughs), but there's absolutely nothing fake about this man. He is exactly what it says on the tin, so therefore I think that when he lets you in, he lets you in.[12]

Finally, the event that took decades to realize and almost nearly had to be canceled took place at the Glastonbury Festival on June 24. It's the biggest and widely considered to be the best annual British musical spectacle. U2 headlined the event and kicked off their set with a blistering, "Even Better Than the Real Thing" and went on stomping through 19 numbers, 17 of which had been singles, before closing with "Out of Control."

The 360 tour came to a close on July 30 in Moncton, New Brunswick, after two years and one month on the road—their longest—and achieving the largest gross of any band in history. Playing near to the town of Springhill, Bono sang a bit of "The Ballad of Springhill" after "I Still Haven't Found What I'm Looking For"—a nod to the mining disaster that hit Springhill in 1958. It was the first time that song appeared in a U2 set since 1987.[13] Bono introduced the final song, "40," by saying, "Thank you for giving us a great life" and went on to pop a bottle of champagne and spray the crowd before leaving the stage.

NOTES

1. "Carla and Bono: 'Intimacy Is the New Punk Rock!'" atU2.com, March 27, 2010, http://www.atu2.com/news/carla-and-bono-intimacy-is-the-new-punk-rock.html.

2. Ibid.

3. "Bono's Top Tips to Being a Frontman," atU2.com, April 18, 2010, http://www.atu2.com/news/bonos-top-tips-to-being-a-frontman.html.

4. "In Ireland, Tuesday's Grace," *New York Times*, June 19, 2010, http://www.nytimes.com/2010/06/20/opinion/20bono.html.

5. "Watch Bono and Edge on *60 Minutes*," atU2.com, November 28, 2010, http://www.atu2.com/news/watch-bono—edge-on-60-minutes.html.

6. "What I Learned from Sargent Shriver," *New York Times*, January 19, 2011, http://www.nytimes.com/2011/01/20/opinion/20bono.html.

7. "U2's Bono Criticised for Endorsing Shoot the Boer Song," BBC News, February 13, 2011, http://www.bbc.co.uk/news/world-africa-12444061.

8. Ibid.

9. "U2 Set to Break Rolling Stones' Record for Highest-Ever Grossing Tour," *NME*, April 8, 2011, http://www.nme.com/news/u2/56005.

10. "There Is Absolutely Nothing Fake About This Man," *Hot Press*, June 2, 2011, http://www.hotpress.com/archive/7927233.html.

11. "Oiler Brule Gave Lift to Hitchhiking Bono," *Edmonton Journal*, June 2, 2011, http://www.edmontonjournal.com/sports/Oiler+Brule+gave+lift+hitchhiking+Bono/4877705/story.html.

12. "There Is Absolutely Nothing Fake About This Man."

13. "U2 Set List: Moncton, July 30, 2011," atU2.com, July 30, 2011, http://www.atu2.com/news/u2-set-list-moncton-july-30–2011.html.

Appendix 1

U2'S STUDIO ALBUMS

Boy (October 1980)
Producer: Steve Lillywhite
Track Listing: I Will Follow/Twilight/An Cat Dubh/Into The
Heart/Out of Control/Stories for Boys/The Ocean/A Day
Without Me/Another Time, Another Place/The Electric Co.,
Shadows and Tall Trees

October (October 1981)
Producer: Steve Lillywhite
Track Listing: Gloria/ I Fall Down/ I Threw a Brick Through a
Window/ Rejoice/ Fire/ Tomorrow/ October/ With A Shout/
Stranger in a Strange Land/ Scarlet/ Is That All?

War (March 1983)
Producer: Steve Lillywhite
Track Listing: Sunday Bloody Sunday/ Seconds/ New Year's Day/
Like a Song. . ./ Drowning Man/ The Refugee/ Two Hearts Beat
As One/ Red Light/ Surrender/ "40"

The Unforgettable Fire (October 1984)
Producer: Brian Eno and Daniel Lanois
Track Listing: A Sort of Homecoming/ Pride (In the Name of
   Love)/Wire/ The Unforgettable Fire/ Promenade/ 4th of July/
   Bad/ Indian Summer Sky/ Elvis Presley and America/ MLK

The Joshua Tree (March 1987)
Producer: Daniel Lanois and Brian Eno
Track Listing: Where the Streets Have No Name/ I Still Haven't
   Found What I'm Looking For/ With or Without You/ Bullet the
   Blue Sky/ Running to Stand Still/ Red Hill Mining Town/ In
   God's Country/ Trip Through Your Wires/ One Tree Hill/ Exit/
   Mothers of the Disappeared

Rattle and Hum (March 1988)
Producer: Jimmy Iovine
Track Listing: Helter Skelter/ Van Dieman's Land/ Desire/ Hawk-
   moon 269/ All Along the Watchtower/ I Still Haven't Found
   What I'm Looking For/ Freedom for My People/ Silver and
   Gold/ Pride (In the Name of Love)/ Angel of Harlem/ Love
   Rescue Me/ When Love Comes to Town/ Heartland/ God Part
   II/ The Star Spangled Banner/ Bullet the Blue Sky/ All I Want
   Is You

Achtung Baby (November 1991)
Producer: Daniel Lanois and Brian Eno
Track Listing: Zoo Station/ Even Better Than the Real Thing/
   One/ Until the End of the World/ Who's Gonna Ride Your Wild
   Horses/ So Cruel/ The Fly/ Mysterious Ways/ Trying to Throw
   Your Arms Around the World/ Ultraviolet (Light My Way)/ Ac-
   robat/ Love Is Blindness

Zooropa (July 1993)
Producer: Flood, Brian Eno, and The Edge
Track Listing: Zooropa/ Babyface/ Numb/ Lemon/ Stay (Faraway,
   So Close)/ Daddy's Gonna Pay for Your Crashed Car/ Some
   Days Are Better Than Others/ The First Time/ Dirty Day/ The
   Wanderer

Pop (March 1997)

Producer: Flood, Howie B, and Steve Osborne

Track Listing: Discotheque/ Do You Feel Loved/ Mofo/ If God Will Send His Angels/ Staring at the Sun/ Last Night on Earth/ Gone/ Miami/ The Playboy Mansion/ If You Wear That Velvet Dress/ Please/ Wake Up Dead Man

All That You Can't Leave Behind (October 2000)

Producer: Daniel Lanois and Brian Eno

Track Listing: Beautiful Day/ Stuck In a Moment You Can't Get Out of/ Elevation/ Walk On/ Kite/ In a Little While/ Wild Honey/ Peace on Earth/ When I Look at the World/ New York/ Grace

How to Dismantle an Atomic Bomb (November 2004)

Producer: Steve Lillywhite, Chris Thomas, Jacknife Lee, Nellee Hooper, Flood, Daniel Lanois, Brian Eno, Carl Glanville.

Track Listing: Vertigo/ Miracle Love/ Sometimes You Can't Make It on Your Own/ Love and Peace Or Else/ City of Blinding Lights/ All Because Of You/ A Man and A Woman/ Crumbs from Your Table/ One Step Closer/ Original of the Species/ Yahweh

No Line on the Horizon (2009)

Producer: Daniel Lanois and Brian Eno

Track Listing: No Line on the Horizon/ Magnificent/ Moment of Surrender/ Unknown Caller/ I'll Go Crazy If I Don't Go Crazy Tonight/ Get on Your Boots/ Stand Up Comedy/ Fez—Being Born/ White As Snow/ Breathe/ Cedars of Lebanon

Appendix 2

U2'S NUMBER 1 SINGLES

U2's Number 1 Singles (United Kingdom)

1988: "Desire"
1991: "The Fly"
1997: "Discothèque"
2000: "Beautiful Day"
2004: "Vertigo"
2005: "Sometimes You Can't Make It on Your Own"

U2's Number 1 Singles (United States)

1987: "With or Without You"
       "I Still Haven't Found What I'm Looking For"

Appendix 3

U2'S VIDEOS

1980: "I Will Follow"
1981: "Gloria"
1982: "A Celebration"
1983: "New Year's Day"
"Two Hearts Beat as One"
"Sunday Bloody Sunday" (live)
1984: "Pride (In the Name of Love)"
"The Unforgettable Fire"
"A Sort of Homecoming"
1985: "Bad" (live)
1987: "With or Without You"
"I Still Haven't Found What I'm Looking For"
"Where the Streets Have No Name"
"Red Hill Mining Town"
"Spanish Eyes"
"In God's Country"
"One Tree Hill"
"Christmas (Baby, Please Come Home)"
1988: "Desire"

"Angel of Harlem"
1989: "When Love Comes to Town"
"All I Want Is You"
1990: "Night and Day"
1991: "The Fly"
"Mysterious Ways"
"One"
1992: "Even Better Than the Real Thing"
"Until the End of the World"
"Who's Gonna Ride Your Wild Horses"
1993: "Love Is Blindness"
"Numb"
"Lemon"
"Stay (Faraway, So Close)"
"I've Got You under My Skin" (with Frank Sinatra)
1995: "Miss Sarajevo"
"Hold Me, Thrill Me, Kiss Me, Kill Me"
1997: "Discothèque"
"Staring at the Sun"
"Last Night on Earth"
"Please"
"If God Will Send His Angels"
"Mofo"
1998: "The Sweetest Thing"
2000: "The Ground beneath Her Feet"
"Beautiful Day"
2001: "Stuck in a Moment You Can't Get Out Of"
"Walk On"
"Elevation"
2002: "Electrical Storm"
2003: "The Hands That Built America"
2004: "Vertigo"
"All Because of You"
2005: "Sometimes You Can't Make It on Your Own"
"City of Blinding Lights"
"Original of the Species"
2006: "One" (with Mary J. Blige)

"The Saints Are Coming" (with Green Day)
"Window in the Skies"
2008:   "I Believe in Father Christmas"
2009:   "Get on Your Boots"
"Magnificent"
"I'll Go Crazy If I Don't Go Crazy Tonight"

Appendix 4

BONO'S AWARDS

2002: Simon Wiesenthal Center's Humanitarian Laureate Award
American Irish Historical Society gold medal for worldwide humanitarian aid

2003: France's Chevalier of Legion of Honour
MusiCares Person of the Year

2004: Chile's Pablo Neruda International Presidential Medal of Honour
King Center's Salute to Greatness Award

2005: Time Magazine's Person of the Year along with Bill and Melinda Gates
Portugal's Order of Liberty

2007: United Kingdom's Knight Commander of the Order of the British Empire
NAACP's Chairman's Award
National Constitutional Center's Philadelphia Liberty Medal

2008: World Summit of Nobel Peace Prize Laureates' Man of Peace Prize

Appendix 5

U2'S AWARDS

GRAMMY AWARDS (22 AWARDS)

1988: Album of the Year: *The Joshua Tree*
Best Rock Duo or Group with Vocal: *The Joshua Tree*
1989: Best Rock Duo or Group with Vocal: "Desire"
Best Performance Music Video: "Where the Streets Have No Name"
1993: Best Rock Duo or Group with Vocal: *Achtung Baby*
1994: Best Alternative Music Album: *Zooropa*
1995: Best Long Form Music Video: *Zoo TV: Live from Sydney*
2001: Best Rock Duo or Group with Vocal, Song of the Year, Record of the Year: "Beautiful Day"
2002: Best Rock Album: *All That You Can't Leave Behind*
Best Rock Duo or Group with Vocal: "Elevation"
Best Pop Duo or Group with Vocal: "Stuck In a Moment You Can't Get Out Of"
Record of the Year: *Walk On*
2005: Best Short Form Music Video, Best Rock Song, Best Rock Duo or Group with Vocal: "Vertigo"

2006: Album of the Year: *How to Dismantle an Atomic Bomb*
Song of the Year: "Sometimes You Can't Make It on Your Own"
Best Rock Duo or Group with Vocal, Best Rock Song: "City of Blinding Lights"
Best Rock Album: *How to Dismantle an Atomic Bomb*

THE BRIT AWARDS (7 AWARDS)

1983: Best Live Act (discretionary award)
1988: Best International Group
1989: Best International Group
1990: Best International Group
1992: Best International Group
1998: Best International Group
2001: Best International Group
Outstanding Contribution to Music

FURTHER READING

Bono/U2 Websites

ATU2. www.atu2.com/

"Bono." *New York Times*. http://topics.nytimes.com/top/reference/times topics/people/b/bono/index.html

Edun. http://www.edun.com/

Elevation Partners. "Bono Managing Director." http://www.elevation.com/index.html

Interference. http://interference.com/

One International. http://www.one.org/international/

Scatter O' Light. http://scatterolight.com/

TED: Ideas Worth Spreading. "Speakers Bono: Musician, Activist." http://www.ted.com/speakers/bono.html

Three Chords and the Truth. http://www.threechordsandthetruth.net/

U2 Achtung. http://u2achtung.com/

U2.com. http://www.u2.com/

U2 Fanz. http://www.u2newzooland.com/

U2 Faqs. http://www.u2faqs.com/

U2 Gigs. http://www.u2gigs.com/

U2 Interviews. http://u2_interviews.tripod.com/index.html

U2LOG. http://u2log.com/

U2 Place. http://www.u2place.com/

U2 Setlist Archive. http://www.u2setlists.com/

U2 Star. http://www.u2star.com/blog/

U2 Station. http://u2station.com/

U2Tour. http://u2tour.de/

U2 Tours. http://www.u2tours.com/

U2 Wanderer. http://www.u2wanderer.org/

Bono/U2 Books

Assayas, Michka. *Bono on Bono*. London: Hodder & Stoughton Ltd., 2005.

Carter, Alan. *Outside Is America: U2 in the US*. Boston: Faber and Faber, 1992.

Clayton-Lea, Tony. *U2 Popaganda: Essential U2 Quotations*. Dublin: Hodder Headline Ireland, 2007.

Cogan, Visnja. *U2: An Irish Phenomenon*. Cork: Collins Press, 2006.

Flanagan, Bill. *U2 at the End of the World*. London: Bantam Press, 1995.

Friday, Gavin. *The Light and Dark*. Utrecht: Von B Press, 1991.

Graham, Bill. *U2: The Early Days; Another Time, Another Place*. London: Octopus Publishing Group, 1989.

Kootnikoff, David. *U2: A Musical Biography*. Santa Barbara: ABC-CLIO, 2010.

McCormick, Neil. *Killing Bono*. New York: Pocket Books, 2004.

McGee, Matt. *U2: A Diary*. London: Omnibus Press, 2008.

Negativland. *Fair Use—the Story of the Letter U and the Numeral 2*. Concord, CA: Seeland, 1995.

Rolling Stone. *U2: The Ultimate Compendium of Interviews, Articles, Facts and Opinions*. New York: Hyperion, 1994.

Schaffer, David. *Bono*. New York: Lucent Books, 2004.

Stokes, Niall. *U2: Into the Heart*. London: Carlton Books, 2005.

Trachtenberg, Martha. *Bono: Rock Star Activist*. Berkeley Heights: Enslow Publishers, Inc., 2008.

U2 by U2. New York: HarperCollins, 2006.

Waters, John. *Race of Angels—the Genesis of U2*. London: Fourth Estate, 1994.

INDEX

About the Author

DAVID KOOTNIKOFF is a Canadian writer and coauthor of *Getting Both Feet Wet: Experiences inside the JET Program*, which won the Japan Festival Award for contributing to understanding between cultures, and *U2: A Musical Biography* (Greenwood, 2009). He is currently working on his doctoral degree in English and Film studies at the University of Alberta, Canada.